COMPACT DISC PAGE AND BAND INFORMATION

MMO CD 3810
MMO Cass. 7068-7070

Music Minus One

SOUSA MARCHES
Plus Others
FOR TRUMPET

Band No. Complete Version		Band No. Minus Trumpet	Page No.
1	*Sousa:* The Washington Post	12	5
2	The Stars And Stripes Forever	13	6
3	*Beethoven:* Military March	14	7
4	*Sousa:* The Liberty Bell	15	8
5	*Schrammel:* Vienna Forever	16	9
6	*Sousa:* Sempera Fidelis	17	10
7	"El Capitan" March	18	11
8	The Gladiator March	19	12
9	*Strauss:* Radetzky March	20	13
10	*Berlioz:* Radoczy March	21	14
11	Tuning Notes - Bb		

T0067817

SOUSA MARCHES
Plus Others

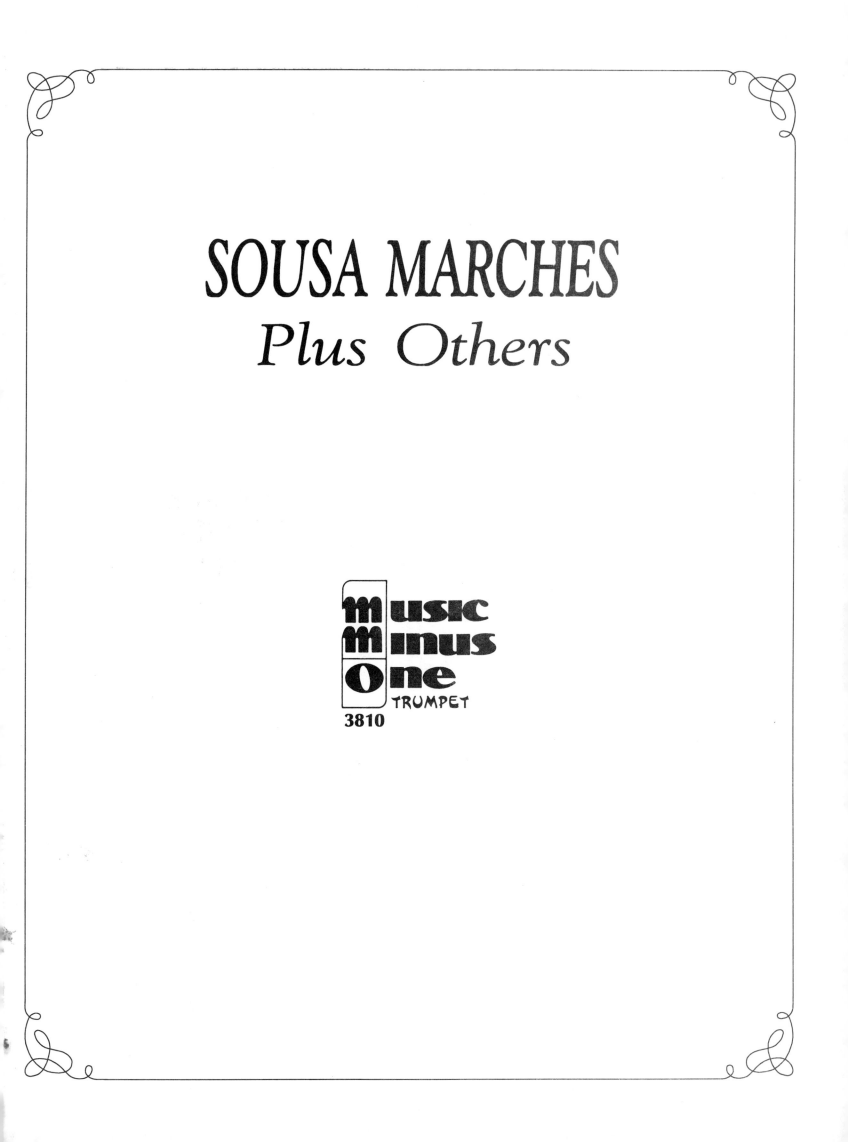

music minus one

TRUMPET

3810

THE WASHINGTON POST

Cassette
SIDE A - BAND 1

Band 1 - With Trumpet
Band 12 - Without Trumpet

Solo B♭ Cornet (Trumpet) or Clarinet

J. P. SOUSA

♩ = 132   playing time: 2:53

D. C.

THE STARS AND STRIPES FOREVER

SIDE A - BAND 2

Band 2 - With Trumpet
Band 13 - WIthout Trumpet

Solo Bb Cornet (Trumpet) or Clarinet

♩ = 132   playing time: 3:20

J. P. SOUSA

MMO CD 3810
Cassette 7070

Cassette

SIDE A - BAND 3

MILITARY MARCH

Band 3 – With Trumpet
Band 14 – Without Trumpet

Solo B♭ Cornet (Trumpet) or Clarinet

BEETHOVEN

♩ = 112   playing time: 1:15

MMO CD 3810
Cassette 7070

Cassette
SIDE A - BAND 4

THE LIBERTY BELL

Band 4 – With Trumpet
Band 15 – Without Trumpet

Solo B♭ Cornet (Trumpet) or Clarinet

♩ = 128   playing time: 3:20

J. P. SOUSA

Cassette
SIDE A - BAND 5

VIENNA FOREVER

Solo B♭ Cornet (Trumpet) or Clarinet

♩ = 100   playing time: 3:20

Band 5 - With Trumpet
Band 16 - Without Trumpet

JOHANN SCHRAMMEL

Cassette
SIDE B - BAND 1

SEMPER FIDELIS

Band 6 - With Trumpet
Band 17 - Without Trumpet

Solo B♭ Cornet (Trumpet) or Clarinet

♩ = 128   playing time: 3:05

J. P. SOUSA

MMO CD 3810
Cassette 7070

Cassette

SIDE B – BAND 2

"EL CAPITAN" MARCH

Band 7 – With Trumpet
Band 18 – Without Trumpet

J. P. SOUSA

Solo B♭ Cornet (Trumpet) or Clarinet

♩ = 128   playing time: 2:08

MMO CD 3810
Cassette 7070

Cassette
SIDE B – BAND 3

THE GLADIATOR MARCH

Band 8 – With Trumpet
Band 19 – Without Trumpet

Solo B♭ Cornet (Trumpet) or Clarinet

J. P. SOUSA

♩ = 132   playing time: 2:30

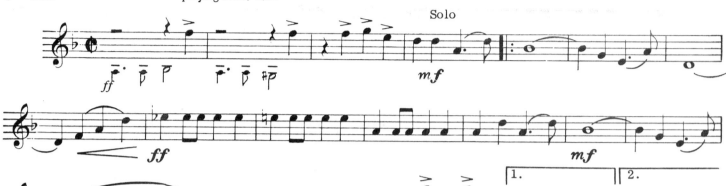

MMO CD 3810
Cassette 7070

Cassette

SIDE B – BAND 4

RADETZKY MARCH

Band 9 – With Trumpet
Band 20 – Without Trumpet

Solo Bb Cornet (Trumpet) or Clarinet

JOHANN STRAUSS, Sr.

♩ = 116   playing time: 2:08

MMO CD 3810
Cassette 7070

D.C. al Fine

RAKOCZY MARCH

Cassette

SIDE B – BAND 5

Band 10 – With Trumpet
Band 21 – Without Trumpet

Solo B♭ Cornet (Trumpet) or Clarinet

BERLIOZ

♩ = 96   playing time: 4:30

Solo B♭ Cornet (Trumpet) or Clarinet

*WORLD'S LARGEST CATALOGUE OF *Participation Records*

MUSIC MINUS ONE • 50 Executive Boulevard • Elmsford, New York 10523-1325

Fall 1995 Catalogue

NEW FALL RELEASES

...and much more

ROCK/POP

ELTON JOHN, THE '95 HITS   PS2326
BLESSED • MADE IN ENGLAND • BELIEVE • HOUSE • MAN

ANNIE LENNOX SONGS, '95   PS2327
DOWNTOWN LIGHTS • WHITER SHADE OF PALE • TAKE ME
TO THE RIVER • TRAIN IN VAIN

IT'S GOOD TO BE SINGIN'   PS2334
HAVE YOU EVER REALLY LOVED A WOMAN? . . . . B. ADAMS
SECRET GARDEN* . . . . .BRUCE SPRINGSTEEN
IT'S GOOD TO BE KING .TOM PETTY
BABY IT'S YOU . . . . .THE BEATLES
DECEMBER . . . . .COLLECTIVE SOUL

IT'S BEEN YOU & THESE SONGS   PS2335
IT'S BEEN YOU . . . . .ANITA BAKER
GRAPEVYNE . . . . .BROWNSTONE
HUMAN NATURE . . . . .MADONNA
MY LOVE IS FOR REAL . . . . .PAULA ABDULE
DON'T TAKE IT PERSONAL . . . . .MONICA

I'LL BE THERE FOR YOU (POP MALE)   PS2345
I CAN LOVE YOU LIKE THAT ALL-4-ONE
I'LL BE THERE FOR YOU . . . . .REMBRANDTS, THEKISS
FROM A ROSE . . . . .THE SEAL
SOMEBODY'S CRYING . . . . .CHRIS ISAAK
WHERE DO I GO FROM YOU . . . . .JON SECADA

ONLY WANNA SING WITH YOU   PS2346
LEARN TO BE STILL . . . . .EAGLES
THIS AIN'T A LOVE SONG . . . . .BON JOVI
HOLD ME, THRILL ME, KISS ME, KILL ME U2
WHAT WOULD YOU SAY . . . . .DAVE MATTHEWS BAND
ONLY WANNA BE WITH YOU . . . .HOOTIE & THE BLOWFISH

YOU OUGHTA SING (POP/ROCK)   PS2347
TOTAL ECLIPSE OF THE HEART . . . . .NICKI FRENCH
RIDICULOUS THOUGHTS . . . . .THE CRANBERRIES
YOU OUGHTA KNOW . . . . .ALANIS MORISSETTE
AS I LAY ME DOWN . . . . .SOPHIE B. HAWKINS
CARNIVAL .NATALIE MERCHANT

HOOTIE & THE BLOWFISH, VOL 1   PS2354
HOLD MY HAND • HANNAH JANE • RUNNING FROM AN
ANGEL • I'M GOIN' HOME • LET HER CRY

HOOTIE & THE BLOWFISH, VOL 2   PS2355
ONLY WANNA BE WITH YOU • TIME • NOT EVEN THE TREES
• DROWNING • GOODBYE

WANNA SING FOREVER   PS2362
I WANNA TAKE FOREVER TONIGHT . . .BERNARD & CETERA
I COULD FALL IN LOVE . . . . .SELENA
HEY NOW (GIRLS JUST WANNA HAVE FUN) CYNDI LAUPER
DO YOU SLEEP? . . . . .LISA LOEB & NINE STORIES
REMEMBER ME THIS WAY . . . . .JORDON HILL

YOU SING THE HITS OF SEAL, VOL. 1   PS2366
I'M ALIVE • NEWBORN FRIEND • CRAZY • PRAYER FOR THE
DYING, A • KISS FROM A ROSE

CRAZY COOL SONGS (FEMALE)   PS2365
RUNAWAY . . . . .JANET JACKSON
FANTASY . . . . .MARIAH CAREY
BROKENHEARTED . . . . .BRANDY/WANYA MORRIS
SAY A PRAYER .TAYLOR DAYNE
CRAZY COOL . . . . .PAULA ABDUL

LET ME SING THIS ONE (MALE)   PS2369
BACK FOR GOOD . . . . .AKE THAT
KEEPER OF THE FLAME . . . . .MARTIN PAGE
WALK IN THE SUN . . . . .BRUCE HORNSBY
SONGBIRD . . . . .D. FOGELBERG & WEISBERG
BLESSID UNION OF SOULS . . . . .LET ME BE THE ONE

ROCK HITS NOW! (MALE)   PS2370
SOMETHING FOR THE PAIN . . . . .BON JOVI
DOWNTOWN VENUS . . . . .P.M. DAWN
JUST LIKE ANYONE . . . . .SOUL ASYLUM
STRONGER NOW . . . . .WARRANT
CRUSH WITH EYELINER . . . . .R.E.M.

WOODSTOCK REVISITED   PS2224
EVIL WAYS . . . . .SANTANA
DANCE TO THE MUSIC . . . . .SLY & THE FAMILY STONE
WOODSTOCK .JONI MITCHELL
NIGHT THEY DROVE OLD DIXIE DOWN . . . . . . .JOAN BAEZ
PROUD MARY . . . . .TINA TURNER
WITH A LITTLE HELP FROM MY FRIENDS . . . .JOE COCKER

LOVE IS STRONG   PS2228
LOVE IS STRONG . . . . .ROLLING STONES
YOU LET YOUR HEART GO TOO FAST . . . . . .SPIN DOCTORS
YOU BETTER WAIT . . . . .STEVE PERRY
FALL DOWN . . . . .TOAD THE WET SPROCKET
THIS COWBOY SONG .STING

THE BIG CHILL ERA VOL.2   PS2233
I HEARD IT THROUGH THE GRAPEVINE . . . . .MARVIN GAYE
YOU'VE REALLY GOT A HOLD ON ME . .SMOKEY ROBINSON
BABY, I NEED YOUR LOVING . . . . .FOUR TOPS
MY GIRL . . . . .TEMPTATIONS
LET'S TWIST AGAIN . . . . .CHUBBY CHECKER

CAN YOU FEEL THE LOVE TONIGHT   PS2226
RETURN TO INNOCENCE . . . . .ENIGMA
ALWAYS . . . . .ERASURE
IF YOU GO . . . . .JON SECADA
CAN YOU FEEL THE LOVE TONIGHT * . . . . . . .ELTON JOHN
I SWEAR ALL-4-ONE

MALE CONTEMPORARY HITS   PS2232
PICTURE POSTCARDS FROM L.A. . . . . . . .JOSHUA KADISON
MISSING YOU . . . . .STEVE PERRY
UNTIL I FALL AWAY . . . . .GIN BLOSSOMS
SIMPLE THINGS, THE . . . . .JOE COCKER
NOTHING LEFT BEHIND US . . . . .RICHARD MARX

CELINE   PS2235
• THE POWER OF LOVE • MISLED • THINK TWICE • WHEN I
FALL IN LOVE • THE COLOUR OF MY LOVE

HAVE A WILD NIGHT   PS2243
SHINE .COLLECTIVE SOUL
WILD NIGHT . . . . .MELLENCAMP & NDEGEOCELLO
I NEED YOUR LOVE .BOSTON
AIN'T GOT NOTHING IF YOU AIN'T GOT LOVE . . .M. BOLTON
THE WAY SHE LOVES ME . . . . .RICHARD MARX

CONTEMPORARY FEMALE HITS   PS2245
YOU . . . . .BONNIE RAITT
DON'T TURN AROUND . . . . .ACE OF BASE
STAY (I MISSED YOU) . . . . . . .LISA LOEB & NINE STORIES
SLEEPING IN MY CAR . . . . .ROXETTE
MAYBE LOVE WILL CHANGE YOUR MIND . . . .STEVEI NICKS

SONGS, ON AND ON   PS2246
THE WOMAN IN ME . . . . .HEART
THE RIGHT KINDA LOVER . . . . .PATTI LABELLE
TELL ME WHERE IT HURTS . . . . .KATHY TROCCOLI
TONIGHT . . . . .XSCAPE
AND ON AND ON * . . . . .JANET JACKSON

LUCKY ONE   PS2254
LUCKY ONE . . . . .AMY GRANT
THINK TWICE . . . . .CELINE DION
GOOD TIMES .EDIE BRICKELL
POSSESSION . . . . .SARAH MCLACHLAN
COME TO MY WINDOW . . . . .MELISSA ETHERIDGE

ENDLESS LOVE - Male Hits   PS2257
ENDLESS LOVE . . . . .L. VANDROSS/M. CAREY
SLOW WINE . . . . .TONY!, TONI!, TONE!
WHEN YOU NEED ME . . . . .AARON HALL
I'M ON MY KNEES . . . . .JONATHAN BUTLER
NEVER LIE . . . . .IMMATURE

ENDLESS LOVE - Female Hits   PS2258
ENDLESS LOVE . . . . .M. CAREY/L. VANDROSS
BODY AND SOUL . . . . .ANITA BAKER
I DON'T WANT TO KNOW . . . . .GLADYS KNIGHT
AT YOUR BEST (YOU ARE LOVE) . . . . .AALIYAH
HONEY . . . . .ARETHA FRANKLIN

CIRCLE OF LIFE & OTHER MALE HITS   PS2259
CIRCLE OF LIFE (FROM THE LION KING) . . . . . .ELTON JOHN
WHIPPED . . . . .JON SECADA
THE LION SLEEPS TONIGHT . . . . .THE TOKENS
LOVE IS ALL AROUND . . . . .WET WET WET
KNOW BY NOW . . . . .ROBERT PALMER

ALL I WANNA DO IS SING   PS2260
ALL I WANNA DO . . . . .SHERYL CROW
I'M THE ONLY ONE . . . . .MELISSA ETHERIDGE
ANYTIME YOU NEED A FRIEND* . . . . . . .MARIAH CAREY
THE COLOR OF NIGHT . . . . .LAUREN CHRISTY
DRUNK ON LOVE . . . . .BASIA

TURN THE BEAT AROUND   PS2261
TURN THE BEAT AROUND . . . . .GLORIA ESTEFAN
RIGHT BESIDE YOU . . . . .SOPHIE HAWKINS
YOU GOTTA BE . . . . .DES'REE
FADE INTO YOU . . . . .MAZZY STAR
AGE AIN'T NOTHING BUT A NUMBER . . . . .AALIYAH

YOU GOT ME ROCKING   PS2267
ALWAYS . . . . .BON JOVI
MOTHERLESS CHILD . . . . .ERIC CLAPTON
YOU GOT ME ROCKING . . . . .ROLLING STONES
ONLY WAITING FOR YOU . . . . .CROSBY, STILLS & NASH
BAD REPUTATION . . . . .FREDDY JOHNSTON

ROCKIN' MALE HITS   PS2268
BREATHE . . . . .COLLECTIVE SOUL
ALLISON ROAD . . . . .GIN BLOSSOMS
DECEMBER 1963 . . . . .FOUR SEASONS
MENTAL PICTURE . . . . .JON SECADA
YOU DON'T KNOW HOW IT FEELS . . . . .TOM PETTY

MADONNA   PS2282
• BAD GIRL • SECRET • THIS USED TO BE MY PLAYGROUND
• RAIN • I'LL REMEMBER

PRINCE   PS2284
• LET IT GO • THE MOST BEAUTIFUL GIRL IN THE WORLD •
PINK CASHMERE • MORNING PAPERS • 7

INTERSTATE LOVE SONGS (MALE)   PS2292
FAR BEHIND . . . . .CANDLEBOX
HOLD MY HAND . . . . .HOOTIE & THE BLOWFISH
SOMETHING'S ALWAYS WRONG . . . .TOAD/WET SPROCKET
INTERSTATE LOVE SONG . . . . .STONE TEMPLE PILOTS
WHAT'S THE FREQUENCY KENNETH? . . . . .R.E.M.

HOLD ME, THRILL ME, KISS ME   PS2293
(IN THE STYLE OF GLORIA ESTEFAN) • TURN THE BEAT
AROUND • HOLD ME, THRILL ME, KISS ME • HOW CAN I BE
SURE • TRACES • DON'T LET THE SUN CATCH YOU CRYING

SING THE HITS OF SHERYL CROW   PS2294
• ALL I WANNA DO • NO ONE SAID IT WOULD BE EASY •
SOLIDIFY • CAN'T CRY ANYMORE • STRONG ENOUGH

SING A SONG OF AMY GRANT   PS2296
• LUCKY ONE • HOUSE OF LOVE w/VINCE GILL • WHATEVER
IT TAKES • OH HOW THE YEARS GO BY • HELPING HAND

MADONNA'S LATEST HITS   PS2302
• SECRET • LOVE TRIED TO WELCOME ME • DON'T STOP •
I'D RATHER BE YOUR LOVER • INSIDE OF ME • TAKE A BOW

HOT SINGING AND DANCING   PS2314
EVERLASTING LOVE . . . . .GLORIA ESTEFAN
SPEND SOME TIME . . . . .BRAND NEW HEAVIES
KEEP GIVIN' ME YOUR LOVE . . . . .CE CE PENISTON
BABY . . . . .BRANDY
MELODY OF LOVE . . . . .DONNA SUMMER

POCKET SONGS CASSETTES

BELIEVE   PS2316
BELIEVE . . . . .ELTON JOHN
CAN'T STOP LOVIN' YOU . . . . .VAN HALEN
YOU WRECK ME . . . . .TOM PETTY
UNTIL THE END OF TIME . . . . .FOREIGNER
BANG AND BLAME . . . . .R.E.M.

LOVE WILL KEEP US ALIVE   PS2317
LET HER CRY . . . . .HOOTIE & THE BLOWFISH
I'M ALIVE . . . . .SEAL
LOVE WILL KEEP US ALIVE . . . . .THE EAGLES
LITTLE BITTY PRETTY ONE . . . . .HUEY LEWIS & THE NEWS
BEAU'S ALL NIGHT RADIO LOVE LINE . .JOSHUA KADISON

IF YOU LOVE THESE SONGS   PS2318
FEEL SO HIGH . . . . .DES'REE
RED LIGHT SPECIAL . . . . .TLC
BEDTIME STORY .MADONNA
IF YOU LOVE ME . . . . .BROWNSTONE
BREAKING UP IS HARD TO DO . . . . .GLORIA ESTEFAN

I KNOW THESE SONGS   PS2319
I KNOW . . . . .DIONNE FARRIS
STRONG ENOUGH . . . . .SHERYL CROW
NO MORE I LOVE YOU'S . . . . .ANNIE LENOX
IF I WANTED TO . . . . .MELISSA ETHERIDGE
LOOK WHAT LOVE HAS DONE . . . . .PATTY SMYTH

COUNTRY

VINCE GILL   PS2280
WHAT THE COWGIRLS DO • I STILL BELIEVE IN YOU • ONE
MORE LAST CHANCE • TRYIN' TO GET OVER YOU • I CAN'T
TELL YOU WHY

HEART SONGS (FEMALE)   PS2324
THE HEART IS A LONELY HUNTER . . . . . . .REBA McENTIRE
YOU DON'T EVEN KNOW WHO I AM . . . . .PATTI LOVELESS
BETWEEN THE TWO OF THEM . . . . .TANYA TUCKER
I WAS BLOWN AWAY . . . . .PAM TILLIS
THAT'S HOW YOU KNOW . . . . .LARI WHITE

ROCK IT LIKE THE TRACTORS   PS2325
BABY LIKES TO ROCK IT • TRYIN' TO GET TO NEW
ORLEANS • FALLIN' APART • THIRTY DAYS • THE TULSA
SHUFFLE

HITS OF MAVERICKS   PS2329
SHOULD HAVE BEEN TRUE, I • NEON BLUE • OH WHAT A
THRILL • PRETEND • THINGS YOU SAID TO ME

I'M STILL SINGIN' WITH YOU   PS2330
I DON'T EVEN KNOW YOUR NAME . . . . . . .ALAN JACKSON
YOU AIN'T MUCH FUN . . . . .TOBY KEITH
I'M STILL DANCIN' WITH YOU . . . . .WADE HAYES
GONNA GET A LIFE . . . . .MARK CHESNUTT
WHAT MATTERED MOST . . . . .TY HERNDON

ONE OF THOSE SONGS   PS2331
YOU CAN SLEEP WHILE I DRIVE . . . . . .TRISHA YEARWOOD
WHEN YOU SAY NOTHING AT ALL . . .KRAUSS & STATION
CLOWN IN YOUR RODE . . . . .KATHY MATTEA
ONE OF THOSE NIGHTS . . . . .LISA BROKOP
ANY MAN OF MINE . . . . .SHANIA TWAIN

SUMMER SONGS ARE COMIN'   PS2332
SUMMER'S COMIN' . . . . .CLINT BLACK
TEXAS TORNADO . . . . .TRACY LAWRENCE
ADALIDA . . . . .GEORGE STRAIT
I DON'T BELIEVE IN GOODBYE . . . . .SAWYER BROWN
IF I WERE YOU . . . . .COLLIN RAYE

THEY'RE PLAYIN' OUR SONG PS2341
TELL ME I WAS DREAMING . . . . .TRAVIS TRITT
THEY'RE PLAYIN' OUR SONG . . . . .NEAL McCOY
BOBBIE ANN MASON . . . . .RICK TREVINO
MISSISSIPPI MOON . . . . .JOHN ANDERSON
SOLD (THE GRUNDY COUNTY AUCTION ACCIDENT) . . . . . .
. . . . .JOHN MICHAEL MONTGOMERY

FIND OUT WHAT'S HAPPENIN'   PS2342
I DIDN'T KNOW MY OWN STRENGTH . . .LORRIE MORGAN
AND STILL .REBA McENTIRE
IN BETWEEN DANCES . . . . .PAM TILLIS
WHY WALK WHEN YOU CAN FLY . . .CHAPIN–CARPENTER
FIND OUT WHAT'S HAPPENIN' . . . . .TANYA TUCKER

SHOULD HAVE ASKED HER FASTER   PS2343
SHOULD HAVE ASKED HER FASTER . . . . .TY ENGLAND
NOT ON YOUR LOVE . . . . .JEFF CARSON
ONE .G. JONES & T. WYNETTE
WALKING TO JERUSALEM . . . . .TRACY BYRD
SHE AIN'T YOUR ORDINARY GIRL . . . . .ALABAMA

THIS IS ME MISSING YOU   PS2344
PARTY CROWD . . . . .DAVID LEE MURPHY
A LITTLE BIT OF YOU . . . . .LEE ROY PARNELL
YOU'RE GONNA MISS ME . . . . .BROOKS & DUNN
YOU HAVE THE RIGHT . . . . .PERFECT STRANGER
THIS IS ME MISSING YOU . . . . .JAMES HOUSE

BABY, NOW THAT I'M SINGIN' TO YOU   PS2350
BABY, NOW THAT I'VE FOUND YOU . . . . . .ALISON KRAUSS
LET'S GO TO LAS VEGAS . . . . .FAITH HILL
HALFWAY DOWN . . . . .PATTY LOVELESS
ONE .T. WYNETTE & G. JONES
I WANNA GO TOO FAR . . . . .TRISHA YEARWOOD

I WANT MY SONGS - MALE   PS2351
WHEN AND WHERE . . . . .CONFEDERATE RAILROAD
SOMEONE ELSE'S STAR . . . . .BRYAN WHITE
I WANT MY GOODBYE BACK . . . . .TY HERNDON
DARNED IF I DON'T (DANGED IF I DO) . . . . .SHENANDOAH
DOWN IN TENNESSEE . . . . .MARK CHESNUTT

I SING ABOUT IT ALL THE TIME   PS2356
ONE EMOTION . . . . .CLINT BLACK
GO REST HIGH ON THAT MOUNTAIN . . . . .VINCE GILL
IF THE WORLD HAD A FRONT PORCH . .TRACY LAWRENCE
BIG OL' TRUCK . . . . .TOBY KEITH
I THINK ABOUT IT ALL THE TIME . . . . .JOHN BERRY

SONGS OF TIM MCGRAW   PS2222
• AIN'T THAT JUST LIKE A DREAM • NOT A MOMENT TOO
SOON • DOWN ON THE FARM • WOULDN'T WANT IT ANY
OTHER WAY • IT DOESN'T GET ANY COUNTRIER THAN THIS
• INDIAN OUTLAW

TAKE THIS SONG   PS2223
DON'T TAKE THE GIRL . . . . .TIM McGRAW
THEY DON'T MAKE 'EM LIKE THAT . . . . .BOY HOWDY
LITTLE ROCK . . . . .COLLIN RAYE
WINK . . . . .NEAL McCOY
THE CHEAP SEATS .ALABAMA

SONGS OF REBA MCENTIRE   PS2225
•I WON'T STAND IN LINE • READ MY MIND • EVERYTHING
THAT YOU WANT • I WOULDN'T WANNA BE YOU • TILL YOU
LOVE ME

LIFESTYLES OF THE NOT SO RICH   PS2240
EVERY ONCE IN A WHILE . . . . .BLACKHAWK
LIFESTYLES OF THE NOT SO RICH . . . . .T. BYRD
TALK SOME .BILLY RAY CYRUS
STOP ON A DIME . . . . .LITTLE TEXAS
THINKIN' PROBLEM . . . . .DAVID BALL

GIRLS WITH GUITARS   PS2241
I TAKE MY CHANCES . . . . .MARY CHAPIN-CARPENTER
GIRLS WITH GUITAR . . . . .WYNONNA
IF YOU CAME BACK FROM HEAVEN . . . . .LORRIE MORGAN
CRY WOLF . . . . .VICTORIA SHAW
INDEPENDENCE DAY . . . . .MARTINA MCBRIDE

MEN WITH GUITARS   PS2242
HALF THE MAN . . . . .CLINT BLACK
DREAMING WITH MY EYES OPEN . . . . . . .CLAY WALKER
WHOLE LOTTA LOVE . . . . .ARRON TIPPIN
WHISPER MY NAME . . . . .RANDY TRAVIS
IT WON'T BE OVER YOU . . . . .STEVE WARINER

BE MY BABY   PS2247
BE MY BABY TONIGHT . . . . .J. M. MONTGOMERY
WHENEVER YOU COME AROUND . . . . .VINCE GILL
FOOLISH PRIDE . . . . .TRAVIS TRITT
I WISH I COULD HAVE BEEN . . . . .JOHN ANDERSON
SUMMERTIME BLUES . . . . .ALAN JACKSON

COUNTRY FALL '94   PS2250
WHAT THE COWGIRLS DO . . . . .VINCE GILL
POCKET OF A CLOWN . . . . .DWIGHT YOAKAM
SHE DREAMS . . . . .MARK CHESNUTT
THIRD ROCK FROM THE SUN . . . . .JOE DIFFIE
WHO'S THAT MAN .TOBY KEITH

THE MAN IN LOVE WITH YOU   PS2251
THE MAN IN LOVE WITH YOU . . . . .GEORGE STRAIT
WHAT'S IN IT FOR ME . . . . .JOHN BERRY
HARD TO SAY . . . . .SAWYER BROWN
MORE LOVE . . . . .DOUG STONE
TEN FEET TALL . . . . .TRAVIS TRITT

XXX'S AND OOO'S   PS2252
XXX'S AND OOO'S . . . . .TRISHA YEARWOOD
SHE THINKS HIS NAME WAS JOHN . . . . . .REBA McENTIRE
I TRY TO THINK ABOUT ELVIS . . . . .PATTY LOVELESS
HEART OVER MIND . . . . .LORRIE MORGAN
WHEN YOU WALK IN THE ROOM . . . . .PAM TILLIS

LOVE A LITTLE STRONGER   PS2255
LIVIN' ON LOVE .ALAN JACKSON
RED, WHITE AND BLUE COLLAR . . . .GIBSON MILLER BAND
THAT'S WHAT LOVE'S ABOUT . . . . .MARTY STUART
WHEN THE THOUGHT OF YOU . . . . .DAVID BELL
LOVE A LITTLE STRONGER . . . . .DIAMOND RIO

SHUT UP AND KISS ME   PS2256
SHUT UP AND KISS ME . . . . . . .MARY CHAPIN-CARPENTER
NOW I KNOW . . . . .LARI WHITE
ONE GOOD MAN . . . . .MICHELLE WRIGHT
NOBODY'S GONNA RAIN . . . . .KATHY MATTEA
WHEN FALLEN ANGELS FLY . . . . .PATTY LOVELESS

SHE'S NOT THE CHEATIN' KIND   PS2264
ELVIS & ANDY . . . . .CONFEDERATE RAILROAD
GOOD YEAR, A . . . . .G. JONES & A. JACKSON
SHE'S NOT THE CHEATIN' . . . . .BROOKS & DUNN
BIG HEART .RODNEY CROWELL
THAT'S WHAT I GET . . . . .HAL KETCHUM

MY KIND OF SONGS   PS2265
HARD LUCK WOMAN . . . . .GARTH BROOKS
CITY PUT THE COUNTRY BACK . . . . .NEAL MCCOY
DRIVE . . . . .STEVE WARINER
YOU NEVER EVEN CALL ME . . . . .DOUG SUPERNAW
WHAT THEY'RE TALKIN' ABOUT . . . . .RHETT AKINS

GIRL THANG (FEMALE COUNTRY)   PS2266
WILD LOVE . . . . .JOY LYNN WHITE
GIRL THANG . . . . .TAMMY WYNETTE/WYNNONA
HERE I AM .PATTY LOVELESS
TO DADDY . . . . .DOLLY PARTON
MAYBE SHE'S HUMAN . . . . .KATHY MATTEA

IF YOU'VE GOT LOVE AND A SONG   PS2269
YOU ARE SO BEAUTIFUL . . . . .KENNY ROGERS
IF YOU'VE GOT LOVE . . . . .J. M. MONTGOMERY
WHEREVER SHE IS . . . . .RICKY VAN SHELTON
SHE CAN'T SAY I DIDN'T CRY . . . . .RICK TREVINO
MAN OF MY WORD . . . . .COLLIN RAYE

THE BIG ONE   PS2270
UNTANGLIN' MY MIND . . . . .CLINT BLACK
MEN WILL BE BOYS . . . . .BILLY DEAN
BIG ONE, THE . . . . .GEORGE STRAIT
COUNTRY 'TIL I DIE . . . . .JOHN ANDERSON
KICK A LITTLE . . . . .LITTLE TEXAS

THERE GOES MY HEART   PS2271
I SEE IT NOW . . . . .TRACY LAWRENCE
IF I COULD MAKE A LIVING . . . . .CLAY WALKER
THERE GOES MY HEART . . . . .THE MAVERICKS
THIRD RATE ROMANCE . . . . .SAMMY KERSHAW
WE CAN'T LOVE LIKE THIS ANYMORE . . . . .ALABAMA

MARK CHESNUTT HITS   PS2274
• LIVE A LITTLE • WHAT A WAY TO LIVE • GOIN' THROUGH
THE BIG D • THIS SIDE OF THE DOOR • RAINY DAY WOMAN
• GONNA GET A LIFE

MARY CHAPIN-CARPENTER   PS2279
• SHUT UP AND KISS ME • HE THINKS HE'LL KEEP HER •
TAKE MY CHANCES • THE BUG • NOT TOO MUCH TO ASK

HITS OF BROOKS AND DUNN   PS2281
• SHE'S NOT THE CHEATIN' KIND • THAT AIN'T NO WAY TO
GO • SHE USED TO BE MINE • BOOT SCOOTIN' BOOGIE •
ROCK MY WORLD

ONCE AGAIN - HITS OF VINCE GILL   PS2289
• WHENEVER YOU COME AROUND • WHEN LOVE FINDS
YOU • YOU BETTER THINK TWICE • IF THERE'S ANYTHING I
CAN DO • MAYBE TONIGHT

THIS IS ME   PS2290
WATERMELON CRAWL . . . . .TRACY BYRD
BABY LIKES TO ROCK IT . . . . .THE TRACTORS
PICKUP MAN .JOE DIFFIE
THIS IS ME . . . . .RANDY TRAVIS
STORM IN THE HEARTLAND . . . . .BILLY RAY CYRUS

WHEN LOVE FINDS YOU   PS2291
WHEN LOVE FINDS YOU . . . . .VINCE GILL
YOU AND ONLY YOU . . . . .JOHN BERRY
DOCTOR TIME . . . . .RICK TREVINO
NOT A MOMENT TOO SOON . . . . .TIM MCGRAW
I SURE CAN SMELL THE RAIN . . . . .BLACKHAWK

GONE COUNTRY   PS2304
NIGHT IS FALLIN' IN MY HEART . . . . .DIAMOND RIO
GONE COUNTRY . . . . .ALAN JACKSON
I'LL NEVER FORGIVE MY HEART . . . . . . .BROOKS & DUNN
HARD LOVIN' WOMAN . . . . .MARK COLLIE
SOUTHBOUND . . . . .SAMMY KERSHAW

SINGING ABOUT YOU   PS2305
MI VIDA LOCA .PAM TILLIS
TENDER WHEN I WANT TO BE .MARY CHAPIN-CARPENTER
THINKIN' ABOUT YOU . . . . .TRISHA YEARWOOD
TAKE THAT .LISA BROKOP
WHOSE BED HAVE YOUR BOOTS . . . . .SHANIA TWAIN

COUNTRY MALE HITS 1995   PS2306
LITTLE HOUSES . . . . .DOUG STONE
I GOT IT HONEST . . . . .AARON TIPPIN
THE FIRST STEP . . . . .TRACY BYRD
MY KIND OF GIRL . . . . .COLLIN RAYE
BETWEEN AN OLD MEMORY AND ME . . . . . .TRAVIS TRITT

COUNTRY MALE HAPPIN'   PS2307
ANGELS AMONG US . . . . .ALABAMA
BEND IT UNTIL IT HURTS . . . . .JOHN ANDERSON
OLD ENOUGH TO KNOW BETTER . . . . .WADE HAYES
UPSTAIRS DOWNTOWN . . . . .TOBY KEITH
THE RED STROKES . . . . .GARTH BROOKS

COUNTRY MALES AGAIN   PS2308
YOU CAN'T MAKE A HEART LOVE . . . . . . .GEORGE STRAIT
AMY'S BACK IN TOWN . . . . .LITTLE TEXAS
DOWN IN FLAMES . . . . .BLACKHAWK
AS ANY FOOL CAN SEE . . . . .TRACEY LAWRENCE
WHEREVER YOU GO . . . . .CLINT BLACK

THIS TIME   PS2309
THIS WOMAN AND THIS MAN . . . . .CLAY WALKER
WHAT'LL YOU DO ABOUT ME . . . . .DOUG SUPERNAW
LIPSTICK PROMISES . . . . .GEORGE DUCAS
WHICH BRIDGE TO CROSS . . . . .VINCE GILL
THIS TIME . . . . .SAWYER BROWN

TRUE TO HIS SONG   PS2310
LOOK WHAT FOLLOWED ME HOME . . . . .DAVID BELL
TRUE TO HIS WORD . . . . .BOY HOWDY
I BRAKE FOR BRUNETTES . . . . .RHETT AKINS
DEJA BLUE . . . . .BILLY RAY CYRUS
BUBBA HYDE .DIAMOND RIO

SONGS FOR LIFE   PS2322
SO HELP ME GIRL . . . . .JOE DIFFIE
GIVE ME ONE MORE SHOT . . . . .ALABAMA
LOOK AT ME NOW . . . . .BRYAN WHITE
SONG FOR THE LIFE . . . . .ALAN JACKSON
LITTLE MISS HONKY TONK . . . . .BROOKS & DUNN

SONGS STAY FOREVER   PS2323
THE BOX . . . . .RANDY TRAVIS
REFRIED DREAMS . . . . .TIM MCGRAW
THE KEEPER OF THE STARS . . . . .TRACY BYRD
STAY FOREVER . . . . .HAL KETCHUM
I SHOULD HAVE BEEN TRUE . . . . .MAVERICKS

SINGIN'...I LIKE IT, I LOVE IT   PS2357
LIFE GOES ON .LITTLE TEXAS
I LET HER LIE . . . . .DARYLE SINGLETARY
THIS THING CALLED WANTIN' . . . . .SAWYER BROWN
I LIKE IT, I LOVE IT . . . . .TIM MCGRAW
SOMETIMES SHE FORGETS . . . . .TRAVIS TRITT

SHE'S EVERY SONG (COUNTRY)   PS2358
SHE'S EVERY WOMAN . . . . .GARTH BROOKS
I'M NOT STRONG ENOUGH TO SAY NO . . . . .BLACKHAWK
NO MAN'S LAND . . . . .JOHN MICHAEL MONTGOMERY
ONE BOY, ONE GIRL . . . . .COLLIN RAYE
I WILL ALWAYS LOVE YOU . . . . V. GILL & D. PARTON

THE SONGS OF LOVE (COUNTRY)   PS2359
BACK IN YOUR ARMS AGAIN . . . . .LORRIE MORGAN
SAFE IN THE ARMS OF LOVE . . . . .MARTINA McBRIDGE
ON MY OWN . . . . .REBA McENTIRE
BETTER THINGS TO DO . . . . .TERRI CLARK
I WILL ALWAYS LOVE YOU . . . . .D. PARTON & V. GILL
THE WOMAN IN ME . . . . .SHANIA TWAIN

ANYTHING FOR LOVE   PS2360
ANYTHING FOR LOVE . . . . .JAMES HOUSE
HEAVEN BOUND (I'M READY) . . . . .SHENANDOAH
THREE WORDS, TWO HEARTS, ONE NIGHT . .MARK COLLIE
DUST ON THE BOTTLE . . . . .DAVID LEE MURPHY
ALL I NEED TO KNOW . . . . .KENNY CHESNEY

KIDS

BEAUTY AND THE BEAST /ALADDIN* PS5513
A Whole New World • Prince Ali • Friend Like Me •
Legend of the Lamp • Be Our Guest • Beauty and
the Beast

SONGS OF HALLOWEEN   PS5514
Ghostbusters . . . . .Ray Parker Jr.
Ding Dong the Witch is Dead . . . . .The Wizard of Oz
People are Strange .The Doors
The Monster Mash . . . . .Bobby Boris Pickett
Phantom of the Opera . . . . .A. L. Webber
They're Coming to Take Me Away . . . . .Napoleon

THE LION KING*   PS5515
I Just Can't Wait to be King • Be Prepared • Hakuna
Matata • Can You Feel the Love Tonight • Circle of Life
• The Lion Sleeps Tonight

KIDS SING THE HITS, VOL.1   PS5516
The Colors of the Wind* (film version) . . . .Pocahontas
Beauty and the Beast* . . . . .Beauty and the Beast
Go Go Power Rangers . . . . .Power Rangers
I Just Can't Wait to be King* . . . . .The Lion King
Hakuna Matata* . . . . .The Lion King
A Whole New World* . . . . .Aladdin
Arabian Nights* (Legend of the Lamp) . . . . .Aladdin

KIDS SING THE HITS, VOL.2   PS 5517
If I Never Knew You . . . . .Jon Secada/Shanice
Can You Feel the Love Tonight* . . . . .The Lion King
We Need a Hero . . . . .Power Rangers
The Lion Sleeps Tonight . . . . .Tokens
Prince Ali * . . . . .Aladdin
Be Our Guest* . . . . .Beauty and the Beast
Just Around the Riverbend* . . . . .Pocahontas
*The Disney company does not permit printing of lyrics.

WIZARD OF OZ   PS 2060
Over the Rainbow • The Merry Old Land of Oz • If I Only
Had A Brain • Ding Dong the Witch Is Dead • We're Off
to See the Wizard

SING A SONG OF MOTHER GOOSE PS 5501
B-i-n-g-o • Three Blind Mice • She'll Be Comin' 'Round
the Mountain • Old Macdonald • Skip to My Lou •
London Bridge Is Falling Down • Oh! Susannah • Are
You Sleeping (Freres Jacques) • This Old Man • Lightly
Row • The Muffin Man • Itsy Bitsy Spider • The Farmer
In the Dell • Reuben, Reuben • Row, Row, Row Your Boat

SING THE HITS!

TAKE ME OUT TO THE BALLGAME PS 5502
Daddy Played First Base • It's A Beautiful Day For A Ball Game • Centerfield • Hit De Long Ball • Willie, Mickey and the Duke • The Umpire • The Animal Baseball Game • Sluggerman • Right Field • Our Old Home Team

LULLABIES PS 5503
Time To/As You Close Your Eyes/Hushabye • All Through The Night • Say Goodnight • Gift of Love • I Love You So • Rock-abye Baby • Starry Skies and Sleepy Eyes • Night, Night • Last Lullaby for Sleepyhead • All the Beauty Everywhere

KIDS SING CHRISTMAS SONGS PS 5504
While Shepherds Watched Their Flocks • Joy to the World • Feliz Navidad • Pat-A-Pan • We Wish You A Merry Christmas • Away In the Manger • Deck the Halls • We Three Kings of Orient Are • Jingle Bells • All I Want for Christmas • Over the River and Through the Woods • The First Noel • Go Tell It On the Mountain • Rudolph the Red Nosed Reindeer • Silent Night • Here We Come A-Caroling • O Come, All Ye Faithful • Santa Claus Is Comin' To Town • Good Christian Men, Rejoice • It Came Upon A Midnight Clear • Frosty the Snowman • Nuttin' for Christmas • Angels We Have Heard On High • Hark! The Herald Angels Sing

WAKE UP YOU SLEEPYHEAD PS 5505
Morning Mambo • Our Secret Rainy Day Club • In the Morning • Wet Your Whistles • Tickle My Tummy • Wake Up You Sleepyhead • One O'Clock, Two O'Clock • Old Man Willikker • Shake and Rattle Those Lazy Bones • Breakfast Sure Is Hard To Beat

PASSOVER SONGS FOR SINGING PS 5506
• Ma Nishtana (The 4 Questions) • Avidim Hayinu • Hin'ni Muchan Dayenu • Ki Lo Na'eh • Adir Hu • Echod Mi Yodea • Chad Gadya • Hal'luya

HANUKAH SONGS FOR SINGING PS 5507
• Y'me Hahanukah • Hanukah/Mi Y'Malel • Sov, Sov, Sov/My Dreidle • Haneyrot Halalu • My Candles • Hanukah Blessings • Ma'Oz Tsur • S'Vivon • Y'ladim Haneyrot • Listen and Follow Me • Ner Li • Kemah, Kemah • Hanukah, Hanukah • Mi Zi Hidlik • Al Hanisim • Shine Little Candles

KIDS SING AMERICA PS 5508
• I Pledge Allegiance • This Is My Country • God Bless America • Erie Canal • Star Spangled Banner • Sweet Betsy From Pike • Yankee Doodle • You're A Grand Old Flag • This Land Is Your Land • Home On the Range • My Country 'Tis of Thee • Pick A Bale of Cotton • Git Along, Little Dogies • Battle Hymn of the Republic • America, the Beautiful • I've Been Working On the Railroad

KIDS RODGERS & HAMMERSTEIN PS 5509
• Do Re Mi • Oh What A Beautiful Morning • Blow High, Blow Low • Dites-moi • I Whistle A Happy Tune • My Favorite Things

KIDS RODGERS & HAMMERSTEIN 2 PS 5510
• Getting To Know You • The Farmer and the Cowman • The Sound of Music • You'll Never Walk Alone • Happy Talk • So Long, Farewell

I TELL YOU, I SAW A MOUSE PS 5511
• Give A Little Whistle • I've Got No Strings • The Mickey Mouse March • Zip-A-Dee-Doo-Dah • With A Smile and A Song • Whistle While You Work • Heigh Ho

TALK TO THE ANIMALS PS 5512
• Talk To the Animals • The Teddy Bear's Picnic • Never Smile At A Crocodile • Itsy Bitsy Spider • Who's Afraid of the Big Bad Wolf • Pink Elephants On Parade • When I See An Elephant Fly • Inch Worm

POCAHONTAS PS2339
• Colors of the Wind • If I Never Knew You • Listen With Your Heart • Just Around the River Bend • Colors of the Wind (film version)

MEET THE FLINTSTONES PS 2237
• Meet the Flintstones • In the Days of the Caveman • Rock With the Caveman • Walk the Dinosaur • Bedrock Anthem

TRICK OR TREAT (HALLOWEEN) PS 5514
• Ghostbusters • Ding Dong the Witch Is Dead • People Are Strange • The Monster Mash • Phantom of the Opera • They're Coming To Take Me Away, Ha-Haa!

SELECTIONS FROM PETER PAN PS 865
• I've Gotta Crow • Never Nrver Land • I'm Flying • Wendy • I Won't Grow Up

A CHRISTMAS PRESENT PS 827
• We Wish You A Merry Christmas • Deck the Halls • The First Noel • We Three Kings Of Orient Are • God Rest Ye Merry Gentlemen • Let It Snow, Let It Snow, Let It Snow • I Saw Mommy Kissing Santa Claus • JingleBell Rock

AMERICA, THE BEAUTIFUL PS 698
• America the Beautiful • God Bless the U.S.A. • Don't Sit Under the Apple Tree • Only in America • America • U.S. of A. • God Bless America • You're A Grand Old Flag

AMERICAN ANTHEMS PS 577
• Yankee Doodle • Anchors Aweigh • Battle Hymn of the Republic • Air Force Song • Marines Hymn • Army Song • The House I Live In • Dixie • This Is My Country • Give Me Your Tired, Your Poor

SONGS FOR SPECIAL OCCASIONS PS 575
• My Funny Valentine • God Bless America • You're A Grand Old Flag • Hail, Hail the Gang's All Here • Easter Parade • White Christmas • Danny Boy • Peter Cottontail • Pomp and Circumstance • For He's A Jolly Good Fellow • Happy Birthday To You • Auld Lang Syne

HITS OF PETER, PAUL AND MARY PS 531
• Puff, the Magic Dragon • If I Had A Hammer • Blowing in the Wind • Five Hundred Miles • Leaving on a Jet Plane

CHRISTMAS ALBUM PS 360
• White Christmas • Santa Claus Is Comin' to Town • Rudolph the Red-Nosed Reindeer • The Christmas Song • Have Yourself A Merry Little Christmas • Silent Night • Blue Christmas • Sleigh Ride • Silver Bells • Home for the Holidays • Count Your Blessing

PATRIOTIC SONGS PS 264
• Star Spangled Banner (H) • America, the Beautiful • My Country 'Tis of Thee • God Bless America • American Dreams • Lift Every Voice and Sing • This Is Your Land • Star Spangled Banner (L)

CHRISTMAS CAROLS (SACRED) PS 202
• Joy to the World • O Come, All Ye Faithful • O Holy Night • It Came Upon A Midnight Clear • O Come, O Come Emmanuel • Hark, the Herald Angels Sing • O Little Town of Bethlehem • Silent Night

CHRISTMAS SONGS (SECULAR) PS 201
• Frosty the Snowman • Winter Wonderland • Twelve Days of Christmas • Auld Lang Syne • I'll Be Home for Christmas • Christmas Song • White Christmas • Jingle Bells

OLIVER PS 89
• Overture • Food, Glorious Food • I Shall Scream • Boy for Sale • That's Your Funeral • Where Is Love • Consider Yourself • Pick a Pocket or Two • It's A Fine Life • I'd Do Anything • Be Back Soon • Oom-Pah-Pah • My Name • As Long As He Needs Me • Who Will Buy? • Reviewing the Situation • Finale   . . .Extended play cassette: $18.00

THE SOUND OF MUSIC PS 76
• Overture • The Sound of Music • Maria • My Favorite Things • Do Re Mi • Sixteen Going On Seventeen • The Lonely Goatherd • How Can Love Survive • So Long, Farewell • No Way to Stop It • An Ordinary Couple • Canticle; Confitemini Domine • Edelweiss • Climb Every Mountain   Extended play cassette: $18.00

WIZARD OF OZ PS 2060
• Over the Rainbow • The Merry Old Land of Oz • If I Only Had A Brain • Ding Dong the Witch Is Dead • We're Off to See the Wizard

PS 698 AMERICA, THE BEAUTIFUL
• America the Beautiful • God Bless the U.S.A. • Don't Sit Under the Apple Tree • Only in America • America • U.S. of A. • God Bless America • You're A Grand Old Flag

FILMS

POCAHONTAS — PS2339
COLORS OF THE WIND (VANESSA WILLIAMS)* • IF I NEVER KNEW YOU* • JUST AROUND THE RIVERBEND* • LISTEN WITH YOUR HEART* • COLORS OF THE WIND*-FILM VERSION

MEET THE FLINTSTONES — PS2237
MEET THE FLINTSTONES . . . . .B-52's
DAYS OF THE CAVEMAN . . . . .CRASH TEST DUMMIES
ROCK WITH THE CAVEMAN . . . . .BIG AUDIO DYNAMITE
WALK THE DINOSAUR . . . . .WAS NOT WAS
BEDROCK ANTHEM * . . . . .WEIRD AL YANKOVIC

MUSIC FROM "FORREST GUMP" — PS2248
TURN, TURN, TURN . . . . .BYRDS
FOR WHAT IT'S WORTH . . . . .BUFFALO SPRINGFIELD
AGAINST THE WIND . . . . .BOB SEGER
RESPECT . . . . .ARETHA FRANKLIN
MRS. ROBINSON . . . . .SIMON AND GARFUNKEL
AQUARIUS/LET THE SUNSHINE IN . . . . .FIFTH DIMENSION

"BOYS ON THE SIDE" - VOL.1 — PS2311
YOU GOT IT . . . . .BONNIE RAITT
I TAKE YOU WITH ME . . . . .MELISSA ETHERIDGE
POWER OF TWO . . . . .INDIGO GIRLS
SOMEBODY STAND BY ME . . . . .STEVIE NICKS
DREAMS . . . . .THE CRANBERRIES

"BOYS ON THE SIDE" - VOL. 2 — PS2312
KEEP ON GROWING .SHERYL CROW
OL' 55 . . . . .SARAH MCLACHLAN
WILLOW . . . . .JOAN ARMATRADING
CROSSROADS . . . . .JONELL MOSSER
WHY . . . . .ANNIE LENNOX

*Printed lyrics not included at publisher's direction

ADULT CONTEMPORARY

THE WEE SMALL HOURS — PS2150
IN THE WEE SMALL HOURS OF THE MORNING • I SEE YOUR FACE BEFORE ME • I GET ALONG WITHOUT YOU VERY WELL • CAN'T WE BE FRIENDS • WHEN YOUR LOVER HAS GONE

THIS LOVE OF MINE — PS2151
I'LL BE AROUND • IT NEVER ENTERED MY MIND • DANCING ON THE CEILING • I'LL NEVER BE THE SAME • THIS LOVE OF MINE

LINDA RONSTADT '95 SONGS — PS2333
THE WAITING • WALK ON • HIGH SIERRA • AFTER THE GOLD RUSH • THE BLUE TRAIN • FEELS LIKE HOME

SONGS BETTE MIDLER SINGS, VOL.1 — PS2352
IT'S TOO LATE TO DESERVE YOU • I BELIEVE IN YOU • I KNOW THIS TOWN • THE PERFECT KISS • IN THIS LIFE

SONGS BETTE MIDLER SINGS, VOL 2 — PS2353
AS DREAMS GO BY • TO COMFORT YOU • BOTTOMLESS • BED OF ROSES • THE LAST TIME

FOREVER TONIGHT SONGS (POP) — PS2361
CAN I TOUCH YOU THERE? . . . . .MICHAEL BOLTON
THIS . . . . .ROD STEWART
TAKE IT ON FAITH . . . . .JOSHUA KADISON
I WANNA TAKE FOREVER TONIGHT . . .CETERA & BERNARD
GO WALKING DOWN THERE . . . . .CHRIS ISAAK

SONGS OF CY COLEMAN — PS2373
• WHEN IN ROME • THE BEST IS YET TO COME • BABY, DREAM YOUR DREAM • HEY, LOOK ME OVER • ON THE OTHER SIDE OF THE STREET

SEND IN THE CLONES — PS2172
YOU'LL NEVER FIND ANOTHER LOVE . . . . .LOU RAWLS
MONA LISA . . . . .NAT 'KING' COLE
TOO CLOSE FOR COMFORT . . . . .SAMMY DAVIS, JR.
COME A LITTLE CLOSER . . . . . .JAY AND THE AMERICANS
MEMORY . . . . .BARBRA STREISAND
I WILL ALWAYS LOVE YOU . . . . .WHITNEY HOUSTON
WIND BENEATH MY WINGS . . . . .BETTE MIDLER
WHAT'S NEW . . . . .LINDA RONSTADT

HITS OF HUEY LEWIS & THE NEWS — PS2227
• BUT IT'S ALRIGHT • SOME KIND OF WONDERFUL • IF YOU GOTTA MAKE A FOOL OF SOMEBODY • SEARCHING FOR MY LOVE • MOTHER-IN-LAW

BARBRA STREISAND CLASSICS — PS2239
• NOT WHILE I'M AROUND • A PIECE OF SKY • THE WAY HE MAKES ME FEEL • PAPA, CAN YOU HEAR ME? • NO MATTER WHAT HAPPENS• ORDINARY MIRACLES

KADISON & COHN — PS2263
WALKING IN MEMPHIS . . . . .MARC COHN
BEAUTIFUL IN MY EYES . . . . .JOSHUA KADISON
TRUE COMPANION . . . . .MARC COHN
JESSIE . . . . .JOSHUA KADISON
MILES AWAY . . . . .MARC COHN

WHISPER YOUR NAME — PS2277
WHISPER YOUR NAME . . . . .HARRY CONNICK
I'M TORE DOWN . . . . .ERIC CLAPTON
FRAGILE . . . . .JULIO IGLESIAS
SKY BLUE AND BLACK . . . . .JACKSON BROWNE
ONCE IN A LIFETIME . . . . .MICHAEL BOLTON

SING THE RHYTHM OF LOVE — PS2295
• BODY AND SOUL • RHYTHM OF LOVE • THE LOOK OF LOVE • YOU BELONG TO ME • I APOLOGIZE • SOMETIMES I WONDER WHY

STREISAND SONGS — PS2238
• GUILTY w/BARRY GIBB • WHAT KIND OF FOOL w/BARRY GIBB • MY HEART BELONGS TO ME • SEND IN THE CLOWNS • BEING ALIVE • WOMAN IN LOVE

THE SWEETEST SONGS — PS2297
THE SWEETEST DAYS . . . . .VANESSA WILLIAMS
DREAM AWAY . . . . .L. STANSFIELD/BABYFACE
WHATEVER YOU IMAGINE . . . . .WENDY MOTEN
LIKE A RIVER . . . . .CARLY SIMON
MOONGLOW . . . . .TONY BENNETT/K.D. LANG

RHYTHM AND BLUES

ALL THIS LOVE (FEMALE) — PS2285
WITH OPEN ARMS . . . . .RACHELLE FERRELL
CAN I STAY WITH YOU . . . . .KARYN WHITE
HIT BY LOVE . . . . .CE CE PENISTON
MAKE IT RIGHT . . . . .LISA STANSFIELD
ALL THIS LOVE .PATTI LABELLE

THESE SONGS BELONG TO YOU — PS2301
OLD SCHOOL LOVIN' . . . . .CHANTE MOORE
EVERYDAY OF THE WEEK . . . . .JADE
I BELONG TO YOU . . . . .TONI BRAXTON
CREEP . . . . .TLC
SHAME . . . . .ZHANE

THIS IS HOW WE SING IT (MALE) — PS2321
GOING IN CIRCLES . . . . .LUTHER VANDROSS
ANSWERING SERVICE . . . . .GERALD LEVERT
THIS IS HOW WE DO IT . . . . .MONTELL JORDAN
RUB UP AGAINST YOU . . . . .FREDDIE JACKSON
DANCE 4 ME . . . . .CHRISTOPHER WILLIAMS

STEVIE WONDER, MORE '95 HITS — PS2328
RAIN YOUR LOVE DOWN • TABOO TO LOVE • SORRY • CONVERSATION PEACE • I'M NEW • TAKE THE TIME OUT

STEVIE WONDER'S LATEST HITS — PS2320
TREAT MYSELF • FOR YOUR LOVE • MY LOVE IS WITH YOU • TOMORROW ROBINS WILL SING • COLD CHILL • EDGE OF ETERNITY

I WANNA SING TO YOU (MALE) — PS2336
CAN'T STOP MY HEART . .AARON NEVILLE
I BELIEVE .BLESSID UNION OF SOULS
I WANNA KNOW YOU . . . . .HOWARD HEWETT
I WANT TO THANK YOU . . . . .FREDDIE JACKSON
WATER RUNS DRY . . . . .BOYZ II MEN
SOMEONE TO SING

TO (MALE) — PS2348
FREEK'N YOU . . . . .JODECI
BROWN SUGAR . . . . .D'ANGELO
SOMEONE TO LOVE . . . . . . .JON B. FEATURING BABYFACE
YOU ARE NOT ALONE . . . . .MICHAEL JACKSON
ON THE DOWN LOW . . . . .BRIAN McKNIGHT

VIBIN' SONGS (MALE) — PS2363
PRETTY GIRL . . . . .JON B.
VIBIN' . . . . .BOYZ II MEN
CURIOSITY . . . . .AARON HALL
'TIL YOU DO ME RIGHT . . . . .AFTER 7
TONITE . . . . .A FEW GOOD MEN

SONGS TO TAKE YOU HIGHER (R&B) — PS2364
TAKE ME HIGHER . . . . .DIANA ROSS
YOU CAN'T RUN . . . . .VANESSA WILLIAMS
LOVE T.K.O. . . . . .REGINA BELLE
WE MUST BE IN LOVE . . . . .PURE SOUL
ARE YOU READY? . . . . .PEBBLES

YOU SING REGINA BELLE,'95, VOL.1 — PS2367
COULD IT BE I'M FALLING IN LOVE • LOVE T.K.O. • YOU MAKE ME FEEL BRAND NEW • HURRY UP THIS WAY AGAIN • THE WHOLE TOWN'S LAUGHING AT ME

YOU SING REGINA BELLE,'95, VOL.2 — PS2368
DIDN'T I (BLOW YOUR MIND THIS TIME) • YOU ARE EVERYTHING • LET ME MAKE LOVE TO YOU • JUST DON'T WANT TO BE LONELY • I'LL BE AROUND

HITS OF VANESSA WILLIAMS VOL. 2 — PS2298
• THE WAY THAT YOU LOVE • HIGHER GROUND • THE SWEETEST DAYS • BETCHA NEVER • SISTER MOON • LONG WAY HOME

CONTEMPORARY R&B FEMALE HITS — PS2229
ANY TIME, ANY PLACE . . . . .JANET JACKSON
BACK & FORTH . . . . .AALIYAH
100% PURE LOVE . . . . .CRYSTAL WATER
DREAM ON DREAMER . . . . .THE BRAND NEW HEAVIES
ANYTHING . . . . .SWV

R & B MALES — PS2231
CAN'T GET ENOUGH . . . . .EL DEBARGE
ON BENDED KNEE . . . . .BOYZ II MEN
THIS LOVE IS FOREVER . . . . .HOWARD HEWETT
DON'T SAY GOODBYE GIRL . . . . .TEVIN CAMPBELL
CAN'T HELP MYSELF . . . . .GERALD LEVERT

BASE/BRANDY/JACKSON/BRAXTON/MADONNA — PS2236
I WANNA BE DOWN . . . . .BRANDY
HOW MANY WAYS . . . . . .TONI BRAXTON
SECRET . . . . .MADONNA
LIVING IN DANGER . . . . ACE OF BASE
YOU WANT THIS . . . . JANET JACKSON

ALL SONGS ARE PERFORMED *IN THE STYLE OF* THE ARTIST NOTED

COMPACT DISCS + GRAPHICS

CONTEMPORARY R & B MALE HITS   PS2244
WHEN CAN I SEE YOU ....BABYFACE
THE PLACE WHERE YOU BELONG ....SHAI
ALWAYS IN MY HEART ....TEVIN CAMPBELL
I MISS YOU ....AARON HALL
I'LL REMEMBER YOU ....ATLANTIC STARR

SWEET LOVE   PS2249
YOU'VE MADE ME SO VERY HAPPY ..BRENDA HOLLOWAY
SWEET LOVE ....ANITA BAKER
LADY MARMALADE ....LABELLE
SIR DUKE ....STEVIE WONDER
HOW SWEET IT IS (TO BE LOVED BY YOU) ..MARVIN GAYE

DO YOU WANNA GET FUNKY   PS2253
I'LL MAKE LOVE TO YOU ....BOYZ II MEN
LET IT GO ....PRINCE
DO YOU WANNA GET FUNKY .....C & C MUSIC FACTORY
WHERE IS MY LOVE? ....EL DEBARGE/BABYFACE
I'D GIVE ANYTHING ....GERALD LEVERT

MALE R & B   PS2272
PRACTICE WHAT YOU PREACH ....BARRY WHITE
I'LL BE AROUND ....JEFFREY OSBORNE/FREEMAN
CAN U GET WITH IT ....USHER
SPEND THE NIGHT ....N-PHASE
WHEN A MAN CRIES ....TONY TERRY

LUTHER VANDROSS LOVE SONGS   PS2275
• ENDLESS LOVE • EVERGREEN • ALWAYS AND FOREVER
• LOVE THE ONE YOU'RE WITH • THE IMPOSSIBLE DREAM
• HELLO

BABYFACE   PS2278
• NEVER KEEPING SECRETS • WHEN CAN I SEE YOU • IT'S
NO CRIME • AND OUR FEELINGS • WHERE IS MY LOVE?

TEVIN CAMPBELL   PS2283
• ALWAYS IN MY HEART • GOODBYE • ALONE WITH YOU
• CAN WE TALK • I'M READY

THE BEST OF R & B VOL. 1   PS2299
BABY, I NEED YOUR LOVIN' ....FOUR TOPS
MY GIRL ....TEMPTATIONS
UNDER THE BOARDWALK ....DRIFTERS
WHAT A WONDERFUL WORLD* ....SAM COOKE
I KNOW I'M LOSING YOU ....TEMPTATIONS
I CAN'T HELP MYSELF ....FOUR TOPS
UP ON THE ROOF ....DRIFTERS
ANOTHER SATURDAY NIGHT ....SAM COOKE

SING THE RHYTHM OF LOVE   PS2295
(IN THE STYLE OF ANITA BAKER) • BODY AND SOUL •
RHYTHM OF LOVE • THE LOOK OF LOVE • I APOLOGIZE •
YOU BELONG TO ME • SOMETIMES I WONDER WHY

YOU SING THE HITS OF DES'REE   PS2313
• YOU GOTTA BE • LITTLE CHILD • CRAZY MAZE • LIVING IN
THE CITY • LOVE IS HERE • I AIN'T MOVIN'

BARRY WHITE'S LATEST HITS   PS2315
• LOVE IS THE ICON • PRACTICE WHAT YOU PREACH •
COME ON • I ONLY WANT TO BE WITH YOU • BABY'S
HOME • SEXY UNDERCOVER

GOSPEL

SONGS OF PRAISE   PS2286
• ROCK OF AGES, CLEFT FOR ME • THE OLD RUGGED
CROSS • AMAZING GRACE • HOLY, HOLY, HOLY • ONWARD
CHRISTIAN SOLDIERS • O, HOW I LOVE JESUS • WHEN THE
ROLL IS CALLED UP YONDER • SWEET BY AND BY • THERE
IS A LAND THAT IS FAIRER THAN DAY

SONGS OF FAITH   PS2287
• HOW GREAT THOU ART • JUST AS I AM • LOVE LIFTED ME
• SOFTLY AND TENDERLY • STANDING ON THE PROMISES •
HAVE THINE OWN WAY, LORD • LEANING ON THE
EVERLASTING ARMS • JESUS LOVES ME

SONGS OF HOPE   PS2288
• GO TELL IT ON THE MOUNTAIN • JUST A CLOSER WALK
WITH THEE • I'LL FLY AWAY • PEACE IN THE VALLEY •
WHEN WE ALL GET TO HEAVEN • PRECIOUS MEMORIES •
HE TOUCHED ME • FARTHER ALONG

CD + Graphics

THE HITS OF DOLLY PARTON   CDG140
ROMEO • YELLOW ROSES • NINE TO FIVE • JOLENE • I WILL
ALWAYS LOVE YOU • HARD CANDY CHRISTMAS • EAGLE
WHEN SHE FLIES • COAT OF MANY COLORS

HITS OF PATSY CLINE   CDG101
I FALL TO PIECES • HALF AS MUCH • IMAGINE THAT •
CRAZY • THREE CIGARETTES IN AN ASHTRAY • SWEET
DREAMS • WALKIN' AFTER MIDNIGHT • SHE'S GOT YOU

COUNTRY FEMALE HITS   CDG102
TAKE IT BACK ....REBA MCENTIRE
SHE'S IN LOVE WITH THE BOY ......TRISHA YEARWOOD
DOWN AT THE TWIST AND SHOUT ..MARY C. CARPENTER
HELP ME MAKE IT THROUGH THE NIGHTSAMMI SMITH
GRANDPA ....THE JUDDS
MEN ....FORESTER SISTERS
LET THAT PONY RUN ....PAM TILLIS
STAND BY YOUR MAN ....TAMMY WYNETTE

COUNTRY MALE HITS   CDG103
AMERICAN HONKY-TONK BAR ASSO .....GARTH BROOKS
I'LL LEAVE THIS WORLD LOVING YOU RICKY VAN SHELTON
T-R-O-U-B-L-E ....TRAVIS TRITT
ALL MY EX'S LIVE IN TEXAS ....GEORGE STRAIT
HERE'S A QUARTER ....TRAVIS TRITT
HARD WORKIN' MAN ....BROOKS & DUNN
CAN I TRUST YOU WITH MY HEART ....TRAVIS TRITT
QUEEN OF MY DOUBLE WIDE TRAILER .SAMMY KERSHAW

COUNTRY MALE CLASSICS   CDG104
ALWAYS ON MY MIND ....WILLIE NELSON
AIN'T IT FUNNY HOW TIME SLIPS AWAY ..WILLIE NELSON
IT'S ONLY MAKE BELIEVE ....CONWAY TWITTY
I LOVE A RAINY NIGHT ....EDDIE RABBITT
THERE'S A FIRE IN THE NIGHT ....ALABAMA
WHAT'S HE DOING IN MY WORLD ....EDDY ARNOLD
GUITARS, CADILLACS ....DWIGHT YOAKAM
HELLO DARLIN' ....CONWAY TWITTY

GREAT STANDARDS   CDG105
I LEFT MY HEART IN SAN FRANCISCO ....TONY BENNETT
OVER THE RAINBOW ....JUDY GARLAND
LOVER MAN (OH WHERE CAN YOU BE?) .LINDA RONSTADT
BUT NOT FOR ME ....HARRY CONNICK
THE WAY HE MAKES ME FEEL ......BARBRA STREISAND
THE WAY WE WERE ....BARBRA STREISAND
NIGHT AND DAY ....FRANK SINATRA
NEW YORK, NEW YORK ....FRANK SINATRA

POP MALE HITS   CDG106
COME AND TALK TO ME ....JODECI
BLAZE OF GLORY ....BON JOVI
REACH OUT, I'LL BE THERE ....MICHAEL BOLTON
ALONE WITH YOU ....CAMPBELL, TEVIN
ADDICTED TO LOVE ....ROBERT PALMER
IT'S SO HARD TO SAY GOODBYE ....BOYZ II MEN
HOW AM I SUPPOSED TO LIVE ....MICHAEL BOLTON
I'D DO ANYTHING FOR LOVE ....MEAT LOAF

POP FEMALE HITS   CDG107
DREAMIN' ....VANESSA WILLIAMS
SAME OLE LOVE ....ANITA BAKER
SEASONS CHANGE ....EXPOSE
A DEEPER LOVE ....ARETHA FRANKLIN
BREATHE AGAIN ....TONI BRAXTON
DELTA DAWN ....BETTE MIDLER
MY LOVIN' (YOU'RE NEVER GONNA GET IT) ....EN VOGUE
BLOWING KISSES IN THE WIND ....PAULA ABDUL

GREAT LOVE SONGS   CDG108
FOR ALL WE KNOW ....THE CARPENTERS
SOMEWHERE OUT THERE ....INGRAM/RONSTADT
I JUST CALLED TO SAY I LOVE YOU .....STEVIE WONDER
YOU DECORATED MY LIFE ....KENNY ROGERS
A VERY SPECIAL LOVE SONG ....CHARLIE RICH
THROUGH THE EYES OF LOVE ....MELISSA MANCHESTER
IF ....BREAD
STOP IN THE NAME OF LOVE ....THE SUPREMES

HITS OF THE 60'S   CDG109
ME AND BOBBY MCGEE ....JANIS JOPLIN
I'M HENRY THE VIII, I AM ....HERMAN'S HERMITS
BABY LOVE ....THE SUPREMES
YOU MUST HAVE BEEN A BEAUTIFUL BABY .BOBBY DARIN
TEARS OF A CLOWN ....SMOKEY ROBINSON
DANKE SCHOEN ....WAYNE NEWTON
SPANISH EYES ....ENGELBERT HUMPERDINCK
EBB TIDE ....RIGHTEOUS BROTHERS

HITS OF THE 50'S   CDG110
AIN'T THAT A SHAME ....FATS DOMINO
THE WONDER OF YOU ....ELVIS PRESLEY
SAVE THE LAST DANCE FOR ME ....DRIFTERS
ON BROADWAY ....DRIFTERS
LOVE IS LIKE A HEATWAVE ...MARTHA & THE VANDELLAS
ONLY THE LONELY ....ROY ORBISON
BLUE MOON ....MARCELS
MY BOYFRIEND'S BACK ....THE ANGELS

CHILDREN'S FAVORITES   CDG111
B-I-N-G-O • ARE YOU SLEEPING (FRERES JACQUES) •
SHE'LL BE COMIN' 'ROUND THE MOUNTAIN • THE MUFFIN
MAN • THE FARMER IN THE DELL • REUBEN, REUBEN • SKIP
TO MY LOU • LONDON BRIDGE IS FALLING DOWN • THREE
BLIND MICE • OH! SUSANNAH • ROW, ROW, ROW YOUR
BOAT • THIS OLD MAN • LIGHTLY ROW • ITSY BITSY SPIDER
• OLD MACDONALD

CHRISTMAS FAVORITES   CDG112
DECK THE HALLS • HAVE YOURSELF A MERRY LITTLE
CHRISTMAS • WE WISH YOU A MERRY CHRISTMAS • WE
THREE KINGS OF ORIENT ARE • IT CAME UPON A
MIDNIGHT CLEAR • JINGLE BELLS • HARK! THE HERALD
ANGELS SING • SILENT NIGHT

7

HITS OF NEIL DIAMOND VOL.1 CDG113
SONGS OF LIFE • SHILO • RED, RED WINE • FOREVER IN BLUE JEANS • DESIREE • BROTHER LOVE'S TRAVELING SALVATION SHOW • AMERICA • SEPTEMBER MORN

HITS OF THE CARPENTERS CDG114
TOP OF THE WORLD • WE'VE ONLY JUST BEGUN • PLEASE MR. POSTMAN • I WON'T LAST A DAY WITHOUT YOU • THERE'S A KIND OF HUSH • RAINY DAYS AND MONDAYS • GOODBYE TO LOVE • YESTERDAY ONCE MORE

HITS OF ELTON JOHN CDG115
CANDLE IN THE WIND • DON'T LET THE SUN GO DOWN ON ME • GOODBYE YELLOW BRICK ROAD • DANIEL • CROCODILE ROCK • BLUE EYES • SACRIFICE • ROCKET MAN

HITS OF BARBRA STREISAND CDG116
AS IF WE NEVER SAID GOODBYE • LUCK BE A LADY • MY MAN • PEOPLE • NOT WHILE I'M AROUND • SEND IN THE CLOWNS • EVERGREEN (A STAR IS BORN) • WITH ONE LOOK

HITS OF FRANK SINATRA CDG117
COME FLY WITH ME • I'VE GOT YOU UNDER MY SKIN • LUCK BE A LADY • WITCHCRAFT • LOVE AND MARRIAGE • ALL OF ME • THE TENDER TRAP (LOVE IS) • FLY ME TO THE MOON

HITS OF ELVIS PRESLEY CDG118
BLUE SUEDE SHOES • JAILHOUSE ROCK • ARE YOU LONESOME TONIGHT • BLUE CHRISTMAS • SUSPICIOUS MINDS • LONG TALL SALLY • AN AMERICAN TRILOGY • CRYING IN THE CHAPEL

WORLD'S GREATEST SING-ALONGS CDG119
THAT OLD GANG OF MINE • MELANCHOLY BABY • PEG O' MY HEART • HAIL, HAIL THE GANG'S ALL HERE • ALABAMA JUBILEE • BABY FACE • I WANT TO BE HAPPY • BYE BYE BLACKBIRD • ME AND MY SHADOW • MOONLIGHT AND ROSES • YOU WERE MEANT FOR ME • YOU ARE MY SUNSHINE

HITS OF BETTE MIDLER CDG120
UNDER THE BOARDWALK • FROM A DISTANCE • THE ROSE • BOOGIE WOOGIE BUGLE BOY • WHEN A MAN LOVES A WOMAN • WIND BENEATH MY WINGS • IN MY LIFE • SOME PEOPLE'S LIVES

BEST OF BROADWAY CDG121
ON MY OWN . . . .(LES MISERABLES)
SOMEWHERE . . . .(WEST SIDE STORY)
WHAT I DID FOR LOVE . . . .(A CHORUS LINE)
ONCE UPON A DREAM (MALE) . . . .(JEKYLL & HYDE)
HELLO DOLLY . . . .(HELLO DOLLY)
HOME . . . .(THE WIZ)
CABARET . . . .(CABARET)
THE DAY AFTER THAT . . . . .(KISS OF THE SPIDER WOMAN)

HITS OF WHITNEY HOUSTON CDG122
I WILL ALWAYS LOVE YOU • GREATEST LOVE OF ALL, THE • LOVE WILL SAVE THE DAY • ALL AT ONCE • DIDN'T WE ALMOST HAVE IT ALL • I WANNA DANCE WITH SOMEBODY • SAVING ALL MY LOVE FOR YOU • LOVER FOR LIFE

HITS OF LINDA RONSTADT CDG123
SKYLARK • YOU TOOK ADVANTAGE OF ME • WHEN I FALL IN LOVE • I GET ALONG WITHOUT YOU VERY WELL (EXCEPT SOM) • 'ROUND MIDNIGHT • BEWITCHED, BOTHERED AND BEWILDERED • MY FUNNY VALENTINE • IT NEVER ENTERED MY MIND

OLD TYME SING-ALONGS CDG124
SOMEBODY STOLE MY GAL • YES SIR, THAT'S MY BABY • OH, YOU BEAUTIFUL DOLL • THE BAND PLAYED ON • THE SIDE-WALKS OF NEW YORK • TAKE ME OUT TO THE BALL GAME • IN A SHANTY IN OLD SHANTY TOWN • HEART OF MY HEART • ALEXANDER'S RAGTIME BAND • MARGIE • MA, HE'S MAKIN' EYES AT ME • PUT YOUR ARMS AROUND ME, HONEY • WHEN YOU WORE A TULIP • PUT ON YOUR OLD GREY BONNET • BILL BAILEY, WON'T YOU PLEASE COME HOME

HITS OF NEIL DIAMOND VOL.2 CDG125
GIRL, YOU'LL BE A WOMAN SOON • HELLO AGAIN • YOU DON'T BRING ME FLOWERS • I AM, I SAID • IF YOU KNOW WHAT I MEAN • KENTUCKY WOMAN • LOVE ON THE ROCKS

HAPPY SONGS ARE HERE AGAIN CDG126
HAPPY DAYS ARE HERE AGAIN (MEDLEY) • I'M SITTING ON TOP OF THE WORLD (MEDLEY) • I'M LOOKING OVER A FOUR LEAF CLOVER (MEDLEY) • MY BLUE HEAVEN (MEDLEY) • SIDE BY SIDE (MEDLEY) • WHEN THE RED, RED ROBIN COMES BOB, BOB BOBBIN' ALONG (MEDLEY) • ON THE SUNNY SIDE OF THE STREET (MEDLEY) • PENNIES FROM HEAVEN (MEDLEY) • SWEET GEORGIA BROWN (MEDLEY) • CHICAGO (THAT TODDLING TOWN) (MEDLEY) • FORTY-SECOND STREET (MEDLEY) • LULLABY OF BROADWAY (MEDLEY) • FIVE FOOT TWO (MEDLEY) • AIN'T SHE SWEET (MEDLEY) • WHEN YOU'RE SMILING (THE WHOLE WORLD SMILES WITH YOU) (MEDLEY)

THE COASTERS & THE DRIFTERS CDG127
SOME KIND OF WONDERFUL • YAKETY YAK • CHARLIE BROWN • SEARCHIN' • POISON IVY • THERE GOES MY BABY • THIS MAGIC MOMENT • UP ON THE ROOF

LOVE SONGS FOR A WEDDING CDG128
INSEPARABLE . . . . .NATALIE COLE
YOU AND I . . . . .E. RABBITT & C. GAYLE
I WILL ALWAYS LOVE YOU . . . . .WHITNEY HOUSTON
ALL I HAVE . . . . .BETH NIELSEN CHAPMAN
BEAUTIFUL IN MY EYES . . . . .JOSHUA KADISON
TRUE COMPANION . . . . .MARC COHN
WHEN YOU TELL ME . . . . .J. IGLESIAS/D. PARTON
THE MAN IN LOVE WITH YOU . . . . .GEORGE STRAIT

MALE CHART TOPPERS CDG130
PEOPLE GET READY . . . . .ROD STEWART
OBJECTS IN THE REARVIEW . . . . . .MEAT LOAF
COMPLETELY . . . . .MICHAEL BOLTON
ENDLESS LOVE . . . . .L. VANDROSS/M. CAREY
BUT IT'S ALRIGHT . . . . .HUEY LEWIS
I SWEAR ALL-4-ONE
YOU LET YOUR HEART GO TOO FAST . . . . .SPIN DOCTORS
YOU BETTER WAIT . . . . .STEVE PERRY

POP MALE HITS CDG131
HOLD MY HAND . . . . .HOOTIE & BLOWFISH
ALWAYS . . . . .BON JOVI
I'LL MAKE LOVE TO YOU . . . . .BOYZ II MEN
SHINE . . . . .COLLECTIVE SOUL
SIMPLE THINGS, THE . . . . .JOE COCKER
YOU DON'T KNOW HOW IT FEELS . . . . .TOM PETTY
I'M TORE DOWN . . . . .ERIC CLAPTON
AIN'T GOT NOTHING . . . . .MICHAEL BOLTON

FEMALE CHART TOPPERS CDG132
ENDLESS LOVE . . . . . . .M. CAREY/L. VANDROSS
LUCKY ONE .AMY GRANT
I'LL REMEMBER . . . . .MADONNA
THINK TWICE . . . . .CELINE DION
YOU MEAN THE WORLD TO ME . . . . TONI BRAXTON
LOVE SNEAKIN' UP ON YOU . .BONNIE RAITT
DON'T TURN AROUND . . . . .ACE OF BASE
THE SWEETEST DAYS . . . . .VANESSA WILLIAMS

POP FEMALE HITS CDG133
TURN THE BEAT AROUND . . . . .GLORIA ESTEFAN
SECRET . . . . .MADONNA
BODY AND SOUL . . . . .ANITA BAKER
WITHOUT YOU . . . . .MARIAH CAREY
STAY . . . . .LISA LOEB & NINE STORIES
HOW MANY WAYS . . . . .TONI BRAXTON
YOU . . . . .BONNIE RAITT,
LIVING IN DANGER . . . . .ACE OF BASE

COUNTRY MALES CDG134
WHAT THE COWGIRLS DO . . . . .VINCE GILL
SUMMERTIME BLUES . . . . .ALAN JACKSON
I SWEAR . . . . .JOHN MICHAEL MONTGOMERY
LITTLE LESS TALK . . . . .TOBY KEITH
I CROSS MY HEART . . . . .GEORGE STRAIT
WE SHALL BE FREE . . . . .GARTH BROOKS
SHE'S NOT CRYIN' ANYMORE . . . . .BILLY RAY CYRUS
PROP ME UP BESIDE THE JUKEBOX . . . . .JOE DIFFIE

COUNTRY FEMALES CDG135
XXX'S AND OOO'S . . . . .TRISHA YEARWOOD
GIRLS WITH GUITARS .WYNONNA
PIECE OF MY HEART . . . . .FAITH HILL
HE THINKS HE'LL KEEP HER . . . MARY CHAPIN CARPENTER
WATCH ME . . . . .LORRIE MORGAN
LISTEN TO THE RADIO . . . . .KATHY MATTEA
SOME KIND OF TROUBLE . . . . .TANYA TUCKER
TAKE IT LIKE A MAN . . . . .MICHELLE WRIGHT

GOSPEL SING-ALONG VOL.1 CDG136
ROCK OF AGES • OLD RUGGED CROSS • AMAZING GRACE • HOLY, HOLY, HOLY • ONWARD CHRISTIAN SOLDIERS • O HOW I LOVE JESUS • WHEN THE ROLL IS CALLED UP YONDER • THERE IS A LAND THAT IS FAIRER THAN DAY 471- SWEET BY AND BY • GO TELL IT ON THE MOUNTAIN • JUST A CLOSER WALK WITH THEE • I'LL FLY AWAY • PEACE IN THE VALLEY

HITS OF NEIL DIAMOND VOL.3 CDG137
SONG SUNG BLUE • CRACKLIN' ROSIE • BEAUTIFUL NOISE • CHERRY, CHERRY • HOLLY HOLY • PLAY ME • SOOLAIMON • SWEET CAROLINE

GOSPEL SING-ALONG VOL.2 CDG138
HOW GREAT THOU ART • JUST AS I AM • LOVE LIFTED ME • SOFTLY AND TENDERLY • STANDING ON THE PROMISES • HAVE THINE OWN WAY, LORD • LEANING ON THE EVERLASTING ARMS • JESUS LOVES ME • WHEN WE ALL GET TO HEAVEN • PRECIOUS MEMORIES • HE TOUCHED ME • FARTHER ALONG

THE PLATTERS CDG139
MY PRAYER • WITH THIS RING • WASHED ASHORE • ONLY YOU (AND YOU ALONE) • (YOU'VE GOT) THE MAGIC TOUCH • SMOKE GETS IN YOUR EYES • THE GREAT PRETENDER • TWILIGHT TIME

HITS OF DOLLY PARTON CDG140
ROMEO • YELLOW ROSES • NINE TO FIVE • JOLENE • I WILL ALWAYS LOVE YOU • HARD CANDY CHRISTMAS • EAGLE WHEN SHE FLIES • COAT OF MANY COLORS

ALL SONGS ARE PERFORMED *IN THE STYLE OF* THE ARTIST NOTED

NEW RELEASES

Compact Discs

RHYTHM AND BLUES

YOU SING REGINA BELLE '95 HITS! CD1202
COULD IT BE I'M FALLING IN LOVE • LOVE T.K.O. • YOU MAKE ME FEEL BRAND NEW • HURRY UP THIS WAY AGAIN • THE WHOLE TOWN'S LAUGHING AT ME • DIDN'T I (BLOW YOUR MIND THIS TIME) • YOU ARE EVERYTHING • LET ME MAKE LOVE TO YOU • JUST DON'T WANT TO BE LONELY • I'LL BE AROUND

ROCK/POP

YOU SING HOOTIE & THE BLOWFISH CD1201
HOLD MY HAND • AN ANGEL • HANNAH JANE • LET HER CRY • I'M GOIN' HOME • ONLY WANNA BE WITH YOU • TIME • NOT EVEN THE TREES • DROWNING • GOODBYE

ADULT CONTEMPORARY

SONGS BETTE MIDLER SINGS CD1200
IN THIS LIFE • IT'S TOO LATE • I BELIEVE IN YOU • I KNOW THIS TOWN • TO DESERVE YOU • THE PERFECT KISS • BOTTOMLESS • TO COMFORT YOU • BED OF ROSES • AS DREAMS GO BY • THE LAST TIME

SING SINATRA WITH STRINGS CD1199
I HADN'T ANYONE TILL YOU • NIGHT AND DAY • MISTY • STARDUST • COME RAIN OR COME SHINE • IT MIGHT AS WELL BE SPRING • PRISONER OF LOVE • THAT'S ALL • ALL OR NOTHING AT ALL • YESTERDAYS

WEE SMALL HOURS (SINATRA) CD1192
I SEE YOUR FACE BEFORE ME • I'LL NEVER BE THE SAME • THIS LOVE OF MINE • I GET ALONG WITHOUT YOU VERY WELL • CAN'T WE BE FRIENDS • WHEN YOUR LOVER HAS GONE • IN THE WEE SMALL HOURS • DANCING ON THE CEILING • IT NEVER ENTERED MY MIND • I'LL BE AROUND

COUNTRY

COUNTRY OLDIES CD1154
STAND BY YOUR MAN • ROSE GARDEN • HARPER VALLEY, P.T.A.• ODE TO BILLY JOE • THESE BOOTS ARE MADE FOR WALKIN' • NINE TO FIVE • JUST ANOTHER WOMAN IN LOVE • BLUE KENTUCKY GIRL • DON'T IT MAKE MY BROWN EYES BLUE • SWEET DREAMS

KIDS

FAVORITE DISNEY SONGS CD1198
COLORS OF THE WIND*• CAN YOU FEEL THE LOVE TONIGHT*• CIRCLE OF LIFE*• HAKUNA MATATA*• I JUST CAN'T WAIT TO BE KING*• THE LION SLEEPS TONIGHT*• COLORS OF THE WIND*• IF I NEVER KNEW YOU*• JUST AROUND THE RIVER BEND*• BE OUR GUEST*• BEAUTY AND THE BEAST*• A WHOLE NEW WORLD*• UNDER THE SEA*

*The Disney company does not permit printing of lyrics.

FILMS

SONGS FROM "BOYS ON THE SIDE" CD1191
YOU GOT IT . . . . .BONNIE RAITT
I TAKE YOU WITH ME . . . . .MELISSA ETHERIDGE
POWER OF TWO . . . . .INDIGO GIRLS
SOMEBODY STAND BY ME . . . . .STEVIE NICKS
DREAMS .THE CRANBERRIES
KEEP ON GROWING . . . . .SHERYL CROW
OL' 55 . . . . .SARAH McLACHLAN
WILLOW . . . . .JOAN ARMATRADING
CROSSROADS .JONELL MOSSE

HITS OF BARBRA STREISAND CD1002
HE TOUCHED ME • MY MAN • DON'T RAIN ON MY PARADE • SEND IN THE CLOWNS • MEMORY • TOMORROW (ANNIE) • EVERGREEN • SOMEWHERE • THE WAY WE WERE • PEOPLE

HITS OF WHITNEY HOUSTON CD1003
• ONE MOMENT IN TIME • I WANNA DANCE WITH SOMEBODY (WHO LOVES ME) • DIDN'T WE ALMOST HAVE IT ALL • ALL AT ONCE • YOU GIVE GOOD LOVE • THE GREATEST LOVE OF ALL • SAVING ALL MY LOVE FOR YOU • SO EMOTIONAL

HITS OF ELVIS PRESLEY CD1004
THE WONDER OF YOU • CAN'T HELP FALLING IN LOVE • STUCK ON YOU • IT'S NOW OR NEVER • LET ME BE YOUR TEDDY BEAR • ONE NIGHT • KENTUCKY RAIN • IN THE GHETTO • MOODY BLUE • IF I CAN DREAM

HITS OF THE BEATLES CD1005
PENNY LANE • STRAWBERRY FIELDS FOREVER • HEY JUDE • NORWEGIAN WOOD • THE FOOL ON THE HILL • GETTING BETTER ALL THE TIME • YESTERDAY • MICHELLE • LET IT BE • ELEANOR RIGBY

HITS OF JANET JACKSON CD1006
ALRIGHT • ESCAPADE • NASTY • MISS YOU MUCH • RHYTHM NATION • CONTROL • LET'S WAIT AWHILE • WHAT HAVE YOU DONE FOR ME LATELY

HITS OF SARAH VAUGHN CD1007
YESTERDAYS • IT'S ALL RIGHT WITH ME • NICE WORK IF YOU CAN GET IT • LULLABY OF BIRDLAND • SPRING WILL BE A LITTLE LATE THIS YEAR • IT MIGHT AS WELL BE SPRING • MOONLIGHT IN VERMONT • MISTY • WHATEVER LOLA WANTS • CAN'T GET OUT OF THIS MOOD

HITS OF ROY ORBISON CD1008
OH, PRETTY WOMAN • ONLY THE LONELY • RUNNING SCARED • CRYING • IN DREAMS • BLUE ANGEL • CANDY MAN • BLUE BAYOU • DREAM BABY • IT'S OVER

HITS OF PATSY CLINE CD1009
BACK IN BABY'S ARMS • HALF AS MUCH • SAN ANTONIO ROSE • FOOLIN' 'ROUND • BLUE MOON OF KENTUCKY • CRAZY • I FALL TO PIECES • SHE'S GOT YOU • SWEET DREAMS • WALKIN' AFTER MIDNIGHT

HITS OF GLORIA ESTEFAN CD1010
ANYTHING FOR YOU*• RHYTHM IS GONNA GET YOU*• CAN'T STAY AWAY FROM YOU*• BETCHA SAY THAT*• CONGA*• WORDS GET IN THE WAY*• BAD BOYS • DON'T WANNA LOSE YOU • HERE WE ARE*

HITS OF BILLY JOEL CD1011
PIANO MAN • IT'S STILL ROCK AND ROLL TO ME • ONLY THE GOOD DIE YOUNG • SHE'S ALWAYS A WOMAN TO ME • NEW YORK STATE OF MIND • TELL HER ABOUT IT • JUST THE WAY YOU ARE • WE DIDN'T START THE FIRE

HITS OF LINDA RONSTADT CD1012
BEWITCHED, BOTHERED AND BEWILDERED • WHEN YOU WISH UPON A STAR • SOPHISTICATED LADY • YOU TOOK ADVANTAGE OF ME • MEAN TO ME • SKYLARKWHEN I FALL IN LOVE • LOVER MAN (OH WHERE CAN YOU BE?) • CRAZY HE CALLS ME • WHAT'S NEW

HITS OF THE CARPENTERS CD1013
HURTING EACH OTHER • CLOSE TO YOU (THEY LONG TO BE) • WE'VE ONLY JUST BEGUN • TOP OF THE WORLD • RAINY DAYS AND MONDAYS • SING • THERE'S A KIND OF HUSH • I WON'T LAST A DAY WITHOUT YOU • GOODBYE TO LOVE • YESTERDAY ONCE MORE

HITS OF DEBBIE GIBSON CD1014
ELECTRIC YOUTH • NO MORE RHYME • LOST IN YOUR EYES • STAYING TOGETHER • FOOLISH BEAT • OUT OF THE BLUE • SHAKE YOUR LOVE • ONLY IN MY DREAMS

HITS OF PAULA ABDUL CD1015
STATE OF ATTRACTION • OPPOSITES ATTRACT • COLD-HEARTED • STRAIGHT UP • NEXT TO YOU • (IT'S JUST) THE WAY THAT YOU LOVE ME • KNOCKED OUT • FOREVER YOUR GIRL

LES MISERABLES/PHANTOM CD1016
• WISHING YOU WERE SOMEHOW HERE AGAIN • ALL I ASK OF YOU , THE THE MUSIC OF THE NIGHT • THE PHANTOM OF THE OPERA • THINK OF ME • BRING HIM HOME • ON MY OWN • STARS • CASTLE ON A CLOUD • I DREAMED A DREAM

HITS OF RAY CHARLES CD1017
WHAT'D I SAY? • I CAN'T STOP LOVING YOU • GEORGIA ON MY MIND • BORN TO LOSE • HALLELUJAH, I LOVE HER SO • UNCHAIN MY HEART • AMERICA, THE BEAUTIFUL • CRYIN' TIME • BUSTED • HIT THE ROAD, JACK

HITS OF NEIL DIAMOND CD1018
KENTUCKY WOMAN • FOREVER IN BLUE JEANS • GIRL, YOU'LL BE A WOMAN SOON • CRACKLIN' ROSIESWEET CAROLINE • SONG SUNG BLUE • YOU DON'T BRING ME FLOWERS • HELLO AGAIN • LOVE ON THE ROCKS • AMERICA

HITS OF ANITA BAKER CD1019
NO ONE IN THE WORLD • CAUGHT UP IN THE RAPTURE • SAME OLE LOVE • SWEET LOVE • MYSTERY • BEEN SO LONG • GIVING YOU THE BEST THAT I GOT • JUST BECAUSE

HITS OF TOM JONES
CD1028
IT LOOKS LIKE I'LL NEVER FALL IN LOVE AGAIN • I BELIEVE • WITHOUT LOVE • GREEN, GREEN GRASS OF HOME • HELP YOURSELF • IT'S NOT UNUSUAL • DELILAH • WHAT'S NEW, PUSSYCAT • LOVE ME TONIGHT • SHE'S A LADY

BOBBY DARIN & FRANK SINATRA   CD1029
YOUNG AT HEART • HOW LITTLE WE KNOW • FOR ONCE IN MY LIFE • COME FLY WITH ME • NICE 'N' EASYTHAT'S ALL • CLEMENTINE • DREAM LOVER • BEYOND THE SEA • MACK THE KNIFE

HITS OF THE FIFTIES   CD1030
HE'S SO FINE* . . . .
THE WANDERER . . . . .DION AND THE BELMONTS
RUNAROUND SUE . . . . .DION AND THE BELMONTS
WHERE THE BOYS ARE . . . . .CONNIE FRANCIS
STOP IN THE NAME OF LOVE . . . . .THE SUPREMES
IT'S MY PARTY . . . . .LESLIE GORE
IN THE STILL OF THE NIGHT . . . . .THE FIVE SATINS
EARTH ANGEL (WILL YOU BE MINE?) . . . . .THE PENGUINS
JOHNNY B. GOODE . . . . .CHUCK BERRY
SIXTEEN CANDLES . . . . .JOHNNY MAESTRO

HITS OF THE SIXTIES   CD1031
LOUIE LOUIE . . . . .THE KINGSMEN
DOWN ON ME . . . . .JANIS JOPLIN
MONDAY, MONDAY . . . . .MAMAS AND THE PAPAS
UNDER THE BOARDWALK . . . . .DRIFTERS
LIKE A ROLLING STONE* . . . . .BOB DYLAN
GOOD LOVIN' . . . . .RASCALS
HIT THE ROAD, JACK . . . . .RAY CHARLES
WHOLE LOTTA SHAKIN' GOIN' ON . . . . . JERRY LEE LEWIS
LEAVING ON A JET PLANE . . . . . . .PETER PAUL AND MARY
LOVE IS JUST A FOUR LETTER WORD . . . . . . .JOAN BAEZ

HITS OF NAT KING COLE   CD1032
MONA LISA • SMILE • TOO YOUNG • UNFORGETTABLE • A BLOSSOM FELL • SOMEWHERE ALONG THE WAY • WALKIN' MY BABY BACK HOME • ANSWER ME, MY LOVE • DARLING, JE VOUS AIME BEAUCOUP • PRETEND

HITS OF THE JUDDS   CD1033
MAYBE YOUR BABY'S GOT THE BLUES • WHY NOT ME? • MAMA HE'S CRAZY • HAVE MERCY • GRANDPA • A GIRL'S NIGHT OUT • CHANGE OF HEART • LOVE IS ALIVE • ROCKIN' WITH THE RHYTHM OF THE RAIN • GIVE A LITTLE LOVE

HITS OF REBA MCENTIRE   CD1034
ONE PROMISE TOO LATE • WHOEVER'S IN NEW ENGLAND • SOMEBODY SHOULD LEAVE • LITTLE ROCK • HAVE I GOT A DEAL FOR YOU • WHAT AM I GONNA DO ABOUT YOU • LAST ONE TO KNOW, THE • CAN'T EVEN GET THE BLUES • SUNDAY KIND OF LOVE • I KNOW HOW HE FEELS

HITS OF MADONNA   CD1035
WHO'S THAT GIRL • PAPA DON'T PREACH • LIVE TO TELL • CHERISH • EXPRESS YOURSELF • OH, FATHER • LIKE A VIRGIN • MATERIAL GIRL

FEMALE GROUPS OF THE 60'S   CD1036
GIVE HIM A GREAT BIG KISS . . . . .SHANGRILAS
LOVER'S CONCERTO . . . . .TOYS
MY BOYFRIEND'S BACK . . . . .THE ANGELS
WALKING IN THE RAIN . . . . .RONETTES
UPTOWN . . . . .CRYSTALS
LEADER OF THE PACK . . . . .SHANGRILAS
WILL YOU STILL LOVE ME TOMORROW . . . . . . .SHIRELLES
OUR DAY WILL COME . . . . . . .RUBY AND THE ROMANTICS
SUMMERTIME, SUMMERTIME . . . . .JAMIES
SUNDAY WILL NEVER BE THE SAME SPANKY & OUR GANG

HITS OF PHIL COLLINS   CD1037
A GROOVY KIND OF LOVE • ONE MORE NIGHT • EASY LOVER* • AGAINST ALL ODDS (TAKE A LOOK AT ME NOW)* • TAKE ME HOME* • SEPARATE LIVES* • YOU CAN'T HURRY LOVE • SUSSUDIO* • IN THE AIR TONIGHT*

HITS OF MALE GROUPS OF THE 60'S   CD1038
A WORLD WITHOUT LOVE . . . . .PETER AND GORDON
BLACK AND WHITE . . . . .THREE DOG NIGHT
DAYDREAM BELIEVER . . . . .MONKEES
DO WAH DIDDY DIDDY . . . . .MANFRED MANN
LADY WILLPOWER . . . . .GARY PUCKETT
MR. TAMBOURINE MAN * . . . . .BYRDS
ONLY IN AMERICA . . . . .JAY AND THE AMERICANS
SUGAR SHACK . . . . .JIMMY GILMER/FIREBALLS
THE LETTER . . . . .BOX TOPS
YOU'VE LOST THAT LOVIN' FEELIN' RIGHTEOUS BROTHERS

HITS OF THE BEACH BOYS   CD1039
SURFIN' USA • BARBARA ANN • I GET AROUND • HELP ME RHONDA • FUN, FUN, FUN • SURFER GIRL • BE TRUE TO YOUR SCHOOL • CALIFORNIA GIRLS • SLOOP JOHN B • WOULDN'T IT BE NICE

HITS OF ANDY WILLIAMS   CD1040
LOVE IS A MANY SPLENDORED THING • MORE (THEME FROM MONDO CANE) • THREE COINS IN THE FOUNTAIN • THE SECOND TIME AROUND • BORN FREE • MOON RIVER • DAYS OF WINE AND ROSES • DEAR HEART • CHARADE • CANADIAN SUNSET

HITS OF SINATRA BRAZIL   CD1041
ONE NOTE SAMBA • ONCE I LOVED • MEDITATION • DINDI • HOW INSENSITIVE • QUIET NIGHTS OF QUIET STARS • WAVE • GIRL FROM IPANEMA, THE • THIS HAPPY MADNESS • TRISTE

HITS OF ANNE MURRAY   CD1042
SNOWBIRD • DANNY'S SONG • SHADOWS IN THE MOONLIGHT • COULD I HAVE THIS DANCE • YOU WON'T SEE ME • I JUST FALL IN LOVE AGAIN • DAYDREAM BELIEVER • JUST ANOTHER WOMAN IN LOVE • YOU NEEDED ME • A LOVE SONG

HITS OF KENNY ROGERS   CD1043
COWARD OF THE COUNTY • RUBY, DON'T TAKE YOUR LOVE TO TOWN • LADY • REUBEN JAMES • THE GAMBLER • SHE BELIEVES IN ME • LUCILLE • WHILE THE FEELING'S GOOD • YOU DECORATED MY LIFE • DAYTIME FRIENDS

HITS OF NANCY WILSON   CD1044
SUPPER TIME • GLAD TO BE UNHAPPY • IN A SENTIMENTAL MOOD • I THOUGHT ABOUT YOU • BUT BEAUTIFUL • GUESS WHO I SAW TODAY? • I'LL WALK ALONE • PRELUDE TO A KISS • THE MASQUERADE IS OVER • HAPPINESS IS A THING CALLED JOE

HITS OF LUTHER VANDROSS   CD1045
CREEPIN' • SINCE I LOST MY BABY • GIVE ME THE REASON • STOP TO LOVE • A HOUSE IS NOT A HOME • NEVER TOO MUCH • FOREVER, FOR ALWAYS, FOR LOVE • SO AMAZING

HITS OF RANDY TRAVIS   CD1046
FOREVER AND EVER, AMEN • TOO GONE, TOO LONG • ON THE OTHER HAND • DIGGIN' UP BONES • NO PLACE LIKE HOME • HONKY TONK MOON • WRITTEN IN STONE • DEEPER THAN THE HOLLER • 1982 • I TOLD YOU SO

HITS OF GEORGE STRAIT   CD1047
AMARILLO BY MORNING • RIGHT OR WRONG • THE CHAIR • ALL MY EX'S LIVE IN TEXAS • OCEAN FRONT PROPERTY • IT AIN'T COOL TO BE CRAZY ABOUT YOU • NOBODY IN HIS RIGHT MIND WOULD HAVE LEFT HER • LET'S FALL TO PIECES TOGETHER • THE COWBOY RIDES AWAY • THE FIREMAN

HITS OF PERRY COMO   CD1048
PAPA LOVES MAMBO • IF • NO OTHER LOVE • DON'T LET THE STARS GET IN YOUR EYES • HOT DIGGITY • 'ROUND AND 'ROUND • CATCH A FALLING STAR • TILL THE END OF TIME • IT'S IMPOSSIBLE • SOME ENCHANTED EVENING

HITS OF ELVIS PRESLEY, VOL.2   CD1049
ALL SHOOK UP • BURNING LOVE • HEARTBREAK HOTEL • ARE YOU LONESOME TONIGHT • RETURN TO SENDER • JAILHOUSE ROCK • HOUND DOG • DON'T BE CRUEL (TO A HEART THAT'S TRUE) • BLUE SUEDE SHOES • LOVE ME TENDER

HITS OF BONNIE RAITT   CD1052
HAVE A HEART • NICK OF TIME • THING CALLED LOVE • LOVE LETTER • RUNAWAY • TOO SOON TO TELL • LUCK OF THE DRAW • I CAN'T MAKE YOU LOVE ME

ITS OF SAMMY DAVIS/A. NEWLEY   CD1020
THE JOKER • TALK TO THE ANIMALS • WHO CAN I TURN TO • A WONDERFUL DAY LIKE TODAY • WHAT KIND OF FOOL AM I • I'VE GOTTA BE ME • THAT OLD BLACK MAGIC • TOO CLOSE FOR COMFORT • THE CANDY MAN • HEY THERE

HITS OF AMY GRANT   CD1021
ANGELS • IT'S NOT A SONG • SING YOUR PRAISE TO THE LORD • FATHER'S EYES • LOVE WILL FIND A WAY • THY WORD • LEAD ME ON • ARMS OF LOVE • WISE UP

HITS OF SANDI PATTI   CD1022
WE SHALL BEHOLD HIM • MORE THAN WONDERFUL • HOW MAJESTIC IS YOUR NAME • VIA DOLOROSA\ • MAKE HIS PRAISE GLORIOUS •SHINE DOWN • LIFT UP THE LORD • SHEPHERD OF MY HEART

CHRISTMAS FAVORITES   CD1023
SANTA CLAUS IS COMIN' TO TOWN . . . . . . .PERRY COMO
HAVE YOURSELF A MERRY LTL XMAS . . ., TONY BENNETT
SILVER BELLS . . . . .PERRY COMO
HOME FOR THE HOLIDAYS . . . . .BING CROSBY
COUNT YOUR BLESSINGS . . . . .BING CROSBY
BLUE CHRISTMAS .ELVIS PRESLEY,
SLEIGH RIDE . . . . .JOHNNY MATHIS
CHRISTMAS SONG (CHESTNUTS ROASTING) . . .NAT COLE
SILENT NIGHT . . . . .PERRY COMO
RUDOLPH THE RED-NOSED REINDEER . . . . . .GENE AUTRY
WHITE CHRISTMAS .BING CROSBY

SONGS OF GEORGE GERSHWIN   CD1024
OH, LADY BE GOOD • EMBRACEABLE YOU • I'VE GOT A CRUSH ON YOU • OF THEE I SING • FASCINATIN' RHYTHM • 'S WONDERFUL • HOW LONG HAS THIS BEEN GOING ON • BUT NOT FOR ME • SOMEONE TO WATCH OVER ME • IDIN' MY TIME • THE MAN I LOVE • SOMEBODY LOVES ME

SONGS OF COLE PORTER   CD1025
BLOW, GABRIEL, BLOW • YOU'RE THE TOP • ANYTHING GOES • WHAT IS THIS THING CALLED LOVE • LOVE FOR SALE • LET'S DO IT • I GET A KICK OUT OF YOU • BEGIN THE BEGUINE • JUST ONE OF THOSE THINGS • YOU DO SOMETHING TO ME • NIGHT AND DAY

HITS OF TONY BENNETT   CD1026
WHAT ARE YOU AFRAID OF • THE GOOD LIFE • A TASTE OF HONEY • MAYBE THIS TIME • WHEN LOVE WAS ALL WE HAD • HERE'S THAT RAINY DAY • I LEFT MY HEART IN SAN FRANCISCO • WHEN JOANNA LOVED ME • THE SHADOW OF YOUR SMILE • THIS IS ALL I ASK

HITS OF DIANA ROSS   CD1027
YOU'RE ALL I NEED TO GET BY • AIN'T NO MOUNTAIN HIGH ENOUGH • WHY DO FOOLS FALL IN LOVE • REACH OUT AND TOUCH (SOMEBODY'S HAND) • UPSIDE DOWN • ENDLESS LOVE • MIRROR, MIRROR • GOOD MORNING HEARTACHE • I'M COMING OUT • TOUCH ME IN THE MORNING

HITS OF GARTH BROOKS   CD1053
NOT COUNTING YOU • THE DANCE • FRIENDS IN LOW PLACES • MUCH TOO YOUNG (TO FEEL THIS DAMNED OLD) • IF TOMORROW NEVER COMES • UNANSWERED PRAYERS • SHAMELESS • RODEO • THE THUNDER ROLLS • TWO OF A KIND, WORKIN' ON A FULL HOUSE

HITS OF HARRY CONNICK, JR.   CD1055
IT HAD TO BE YOU • OUR LOVE IS HERE TO STAY • BUT NOT FOR ME • DON'T GET AROUND MUCH ANYMORE • LET'S CALL THE WHOLE THING OFF • WE ARE IN LOVE • FOREVER, FOR NOW • RECIPE FOR LOVE • IT'S ALL RIGHT WITH ME • I COULD WRITE A BOOK

HITS OF BETTE MIDLER   CD1056
SPRING CAN REALLY HANG YOU UP THE MOST • FROM A DISTANCE • DO YOU WANNA DANCE • THE GLORY OF LOVE • THE ROSE • BOOGIE WOOGIE BUGLE BOY • WIND BENEATH MY WINGS • UNDER THE BOARDWALK • IN MY LIFE

ELVIS PRESLEY - THE SUN YEARS   CD1057
THAT'S ALL RIGHT • BLUE MOON OF KENTUCKY • GOOD ROCKIN' TONIGHT • I LOVE YOU BECAUSE • JUST BECAUSE • BABY, LET'S PLAY HOUSE • I DON'T CARE IF THE SUN DON'T SHINE • I'M LEFT, YOU'RE RIGHT, SHE'S GONE • TOMORROW NIGHT • HARBOR LIGHTS

HITS OF RICHARD MARX   CD1058
SATISFIED • RIGHT HERE WAITING • TAKE THIS HEART • ANGELIA • DON'T MEAN NOTHING" ENDLESS SUMMER NIGHTS • HAZARD • HOLD ON TO THE NIGHTS

HITS OF QUEEN   CD1059
CRAZY LITTLE THING CALLED LOVE • ANOTHER ONE BITES THE DUST • WE ARE THE CHAMPIONS • RADIO GA-GA • SHOW MUST GO ON, THE • BOHEMIAN RHAPSODY • KIND OF MAGIC • THE MIRACLE • I WANT IT ALL

HITS OF TINA TURNER   CD1060
WHAT'S LOVE GOT TO DO WITH IT • PRIVATE DANCER • WE DON'T NEED ANOTHER HERO • BEST, THE • TYPICAL MALE • TWO PEOPLE • LET'S STAY TOGETHER • RIVER DEEP, MOUNTAIN HIGH * • PROUD MARY

HITS OF ELTON JOHN   CD1061
GOODBYE YELLOW BRICK ROAD • DON'T LET THE SUN GO DOWN ON ME • CANDLE IN THE WIND • ROCKET MAN • BLUE EYES • SACRIFICE • DANIEL • NIKITA

ROCK AND METAL BALLADS   CD1062
WIND OF CHANGE . . . . .SCORPIONS
(EVERYTHING I DO) I DO IT FOR YOU . . . . .BRYAN ADAMS,
IS THIS LOVE . . . . .WHITESNAKE
DON'T CRY . . . . .GUNS 'N' ROSES
CARRIE . . . . .EUROPE
SWEET CHILD O' MINE . . . . .GUNS 'N' ROSES
I WANT TO KNOW WHAT LOVE IS . . . . .FOREIGNER
RIGHT HERE WAITING . . . . .RICHARD MARX

HITS OF MICHAEL JACKSON   CD1063
BEAT IT • BILLIE JEAN • ROCK WITH YOU • WANNA BE STARTIN' SOMETHIN' • DON'T STOP TILL YOU GET ENOUGH • DIRTY DIANA • ANOTHER PART OF ME • MAN IN THE MIRROR • BAD

HITS OF ROD STEWART   CD1064
DO YA THINK I'M SEXY • MAGGIE MAY • TONIGHT'S THE NIGHT • FOREVER YOUNG • YOU'RE IN MY HEART (THE FINAL ACCLAIM) • DOWNTOWN TRAIN • MY HEART CAN'T TELL YOU NO • THE MOTOWN SONG

HITS OF ENGELBERT HUMPERDINCK   CD1065
ANOTHER PLACE, ANOTHER TIME • RELEASE ME (AND LET ME LOVE AGAIN) • WINTER WORLD OF LOVE • AM I THAT EASY TO FORGET • TILL • AFTER THE LOVIN' • SPANISH EYES • A MAN WITHOUT LOVE • QUANDO, QUANDO, QUANDO • THE WAY IT USED TO BE

HITS OF ROCK AND ROLL MUSIC   CD1066
ROCK AROUND THE CLOCK . . .BILL HALEY & THE COMETS
TUTTI-FRUTTI . . . . .LITTLE RICHARD
ROCK AND ROLL MUSIC . . . . .CHUCK BERRY
BLUE SUEDE SHOES . . . . .ELVIS PRESLEY
I'M WALKIN' . . . . .FATS DOMINO
BLUEBERRY HILL . . . . .FATS DOMINO
GREAT BALLS OF FIRE . . . . . . .JERRY LEE LEWIS
SUMMERTIME BLUES . . . .
. . . . . . .EDDIE COCHRAN . . . . .
LET'S TWIST AGAIN . . . . .
. . . . . . .CHUBBY CHECKER
SWEET LITTLE SIXTEEN . . .
. . . . .CHUCK BERRY

HITS OF NEIL DIAMOND VOL. 2   CD1068
CHERRY, CHERRY • SHILO • I'M A BELIEVER • BROTHER LOVE'S TRAVELING SALVATION SHOW • IF YOU KNOW WHAT I MEAN • SOLITARY MAN • SONGS OF LIFE • SOOLAIMON • PLAY ME • HOLLY HOLY

HITS OF IRVING BERLIN   CD1069
LET'S FACE THE MUSIC AND DANCE • CHANGE PARTNERS • STEPPIN' OUT WITH MY BABY • CHEEK TO CHEEKTOP HAT, WHITE TIE AND TAILS • LET YOURSELF GO • SAY IT ISN'T SO • ISN'T THIS A LOVELY DAY • THIS YEAR'S KISSES • BE CAREFUL IT'S MY HEART

SONGS OF THE ISLANDS   CD1070
THE HAWAIIAN WEDDING SONG • SONG OF THE ISLAND • A SONG OF OLD HAWAII • BEYOND THE REEF • HAWAIIAN OE (FAREWELL TO THEE) • THE MOON OF MANAKOORA • TO YOU SWEETHEART, ALOHA • BLUE HAWAII • I'LL WEAVE A LEI OF STARS FOR YOU • SWEET LEILANI

KARAOKE PARTY   CD1071
WIND OF CHANGE . . . . .SCORPIONS
(EVERYTHING I DO) I DO IT FOR YOU . . . . .BRYAN ADAMS,
THE ROSE . . . . .BETTE MIDLER
ROCK AROUND THE CLOCK . . .BILL HALEY & THE COMETS
MEMORY * . . . . .BARBRA STREISAND
LIKE A VIRGIN . . . . .MADONNA
NEW YORK, NEW YORK . . . . .FRANK SINATRA
ONE MOMENT IN TIME . . . .,WHITNEY HOUSTON
WHAT'S LOVE GOT TO DO WITH IT . . . . .TINA TURNER,

HITS OF JAMES TAYLOR   CD1072
NEVER DIE YOUNG • SWEET POTATO PIE • COUNTRY ROAD • UP ON THE ROOF • LIKE EVERYONE SHE KNOWS • DON'T LET ME BE LONELY TONIGHT • HOW SWEET IT IS (TO BE LOVED BY YOU) • HANDY MAN • FIRE AND RAIN • YOU'VE GOT A FRIEND

CONTEMPORARY RHYTHM & BLUES   CD1073
SLOW DANCE (HEY MR. DJ) . . .R. KELLY/PUBLIC ANNOUNC
ALONE WITH YOU . . . . .TEVIN CAMPBELL
KICKIN' IT . . . . .AFTER 7
CAN YOU HANDLE IT? . . . . .GERALD LEVERT
MONEY CAN'T BUY YOU LOVE . . . . . . .RALPH TRESVANT
I'VE BEEN SEARCHIN' . . . . .GLENN JONES,
HONEY LOVE/R KELLY. . . . . .PUBLIC ANNOUNC
GOODBYE . . . . .TEVIN CAMPBELL

ELVIS AT THE MOVIES   CD1074
VIVA LAS VEGAS • PUPPET ON A STRING (GIRL HAPPY) • SEPARATE WAYS • FOLLOW THAT DREAM • KISSIN' COUSINS • MEMORIES • DON'T CRY DADDY • IT'S OVER • WEAR MY RING AROUND YOUR NECK • HOME IS WHERE THE HEART IS • PLEASE DON'T STOP LOVING ME

HITS OF MATT MONRO   CD1076
COME BACK TO ME • YOU'VE GOT POSSIBILITIES • REAL LIVE GIRL • I'LL TAKE ROMANCE • IF SHE WALKED INTO MY LIFE • PORTRAIT OF MY LOVE, A • ON A CLEAR DAY • AROUND THE WORLD • SOFTLY AS I LEAVE YOU • MY KIND OF GIRL • WEDNESDAY'S CHILD

SONGS OF HAROLD ARLEN   CD1077
MY SHINING HOUR • THE BLUES IN THE NIGHT • I'VE GOT THE WORLD ON A STRING • COME RAIN OR COME SHINE • STORMY WEATHER • I GOTTA RIGHT TO SING THE BLUES • OUT OF THIS WORLD • HOORAY FOR LOVE • DOWN WITH LOVE • AS LONG AS I LIVE

GREAT STANDARDS   CD1078
A HUNDRED YEARS FROM TODAY • MANHATTAN • GHOST OF A CHANCE • SUGAR • DON'T BLAME ME • EAST OF THE SUN • DOWN WITH LOVE • A WOMAN'S INTUITION • OH, LOOK AT ME NOW • STARS FELL ON ALABAMA • SWEET AND LOWDOWN

HITS OF WHITNEY HOUSTON, VOL.2   CD1079
WHERE DO BROKEN HEARTS GO • YOU'RE STILL MY MAN • LOVE WILL SAVE THE DAY • QUEEN OF THE NIGHT • RUN TO YOU • I HAVE NOTHING • I WILL ALWAYS LOVE YOU • I'M EVERY WOMAN

BING, BOB & ASTAIRE   CD1080
ROAD TO MOROCCO • TRUE LOVE • ISN'T THIS A LOVELY DAY • WELL, DID YOU EVAH? • THANKS FOR THE MEMORY • PUT IT THERE, PAL • TWO SLEEPY PEOPLE • MERRY-GO-RUN-AROUND, THE • TEA FOR TWO • YOU'RE THE TOP

PEABO BRYSON & BOBBY BROWN   CD1081
WHOLE NEW WORLD, A * • CAN YOU STOP THE RAIN • IF EVER YOU'RE IN MY ARMS AGAIN • SOMETHING IN COMMON • I'M YOUR FRIEND • EVERY LITTLE STEP • MY PREROGATIVE • BEAUTY AND THE BEAST *

SONGS FOR A WEDDING   CD1083
UP WHERE WE BELONG . . . . .JOE COCKER
SOMEWHERE OUT THERE . . . . .INGRAM/RONSTADT
DON'T KNOW MUCH . . . . .NEVILLE/RONSTADT
THROUGH THE YEARS . . . . .KENNY ROGERS
YOU'RE MY EVERYTHING . . . . .SANTA ESMERALDA
WEDDING MARCH (RECESSIONAL) .FELIX MENDELSSOHN
LONGERDAN . . . . .FOGELBERG
ONE HAND, ONE HEART . . . .(WEST SIDE STORY)
THROUGH THE EYES OF LOVE . . . .(ICE CASTLES)
AND I LOVE YOU SO .PAUL ANKA
THERE IS LOVE (WEDDING SONG) . . . . . . .PAUL STOOKEY

SONGS FOR A WEDDING, VOL. 2   CD1084
WIND BENEATH MY WINGS . . . . .BETTE MIDLER
ALWAYS . . . . .ATLANTIC STARR
THE ROSE . . . . .BETTE MIDLER
YOU TAKE MY BREATH AWAY . . . . .BERLIN
ON THE WINGS OF LOVE . . . . .JEFFREY OSBOURNE
THE GREATEST LOVE OF ALL . . . . . . .WHITNEY HOUSTON
COULD I HAVE THIS DANCE . . . . .ANNE MURRAY
WE'VE ONLY JUST BEGUN . . . . .CARPENTERS
DADDY'S LITTLE GIRL . . . .(STANDARD)
SOMEWHERE . . . . .BARBRA STREISAND

HITS OF MICHAEL BOLTON   CD1085

HITS OF MICHAEL BOLTON — CD1085
(SITTIN' ON) THE DOCK OF THE BAY • HOW AM I SUPPOSED TO LIVE WITHOUT YOU • .SOUL PROVIDER • YOU SEND ME • DRIFT AWAY • KNOCK ON WOOD • SINCE I FELL FOR YOU • TO LOVE SOMEBODY • REACH OUT, I'LL BE THERE

CONTEMPORARY MALE HITS OF THE 90'S — CD1086
(EVERYTHING I DO) I DO IT FOR YOU ..... BRYAN ADAMS
THE CRYING GAME ....BOY GEORGE
A WHOLE NEW WORLD* ....BRYSON/BELLE
GET AWAY ....BOBBY BROWN
IF I EVER LOSE MY FAITH IN YOU ....STING
ORDINARY WORLD ....DURAN DURAN
ANGEL ....JON SECADA
TO LOVE SOMEBODY ....MICHAEL BOLTON

FEMALE HITS OF THE 90'S — CD1087
NO ORDINARY LOVE ....SADE
I WILL ALWAYS LOVE YOU ....WHITNEY HOUSTON
LOVE IS ....MCKNIGHT/WILLIAMS
LOVE CAN MOVE MOUNTAINS ....CELINE DION
WORK TO DO ....VANESSA WILLIAMS
I SEE YOUR SMILE* ....GLORIA ESTEFAN
I'M EVERY WOMAN ....WHITNEY HOUSTON
GIVE IT UP, TURN IT LOOSE ....EN VOGUE

D.J. PARTY — CD1088
STROKIN' ....
...CLARENCE CARTER
RED, RED WINE ...UB40
JAMMING ....
........BOB MARLEY
TOGETHER FOREVER ....
.......RICK ASTLEY
CONGA* ....
. MIAMI SOUND MACHINE
ELECTRIC SLIDE ....
......MARCIA GRIFFITH
CELEBRATION ....
...KOOL AND THE GANG
LIMBO ROCK ....CHUBBY CHECKER
SHOUT! ....ISLEY BROTHERS
HOT, HOT, HOT ....BUSTER POINDEXTER

SONGBIRDS - FEMALE COUNTRY — CD1089
PASSIONATE KISSES ....MARY-CHAPIN CARPENTER
WHAT PART OF NO? ....LORRIE MORGAN
LET THAT PONY RUN ....PAM TILLIS
IT'S A LITTLE TOO LATE ....TANYA TUCKER
OH LONESOME YOU ....TRISHA YEARWOOD
THE TIME HAS COME ....MARTINA MCBRIDE
NIGHT THE LIGHTS WENT OUT IN GEORGIA ..R. MCENTIRE
HONKY TONK BABY ....HIGHWAY 101
A LITTLE BIT OF LOVE ....WYNONNA
SOMEWHERE BETWEEN ....SUZY BOGGUSS

COUNTRY KARAOKE — CD1090
I SAW THE LIGHT ....WYNONNA
DRIVE SOUTH ....SUZY BOGGUSS
SOMETHING IN RED ....LORRIE MORGAN
SHAKE THE SUGAR TREE ....PAM TILLIS
AS LONG AS YOU BELONG TO ME ....HOLLY DUNN
THAT'S ME ....MARTINA MCBRIDE
TAKE IT BACK ....REBA MCENTIRE
HE WOULD BE SIXTEEN ....MICHELLE WRIGHT
TWO SPARROWS IN A HURRICANE ....TANYA TUCKER
WALKAWAY JOE ....TRISHA YEARWOOD

COUNTRY KARAOKE — CD1091
I STILL BELIEVE IN YOU ....VINCE GILL
LORD HAVE MERCY ON THE WORKING MAN ....
.................................TRAVIS TRITT
WHATCHA GONNA DO WITH A COWBOY .CHRIS LEDOUX
SO MUCH LIKE MY DAD ....GEORGE STRAIT
LOVE'S GOT A HOLD ON YOU ....ALAN JACKSON
THE RIVER ....GARTH BROOKS
WHEN IT COMES TO YOU ....JOHN ANDERSON
COME IN OUT OF THE PAIN ....DOUG STONE
BILLY THE KID ....BILLY DEAN
ACHY BREAKY HEART ....BILLY RAY CYRUS

COUNTRY LADIES — CD1092
IS THERE LIFE OUT THERE?* ....REBA MCENTIRE
LONESOME STANDARD TIME ....KATHY MATTEA
WATCH ME ....LORRIE MORGAN
LETTING GO ....SUZY BOGGUSS
NOT TOO MUCH TO ASK ......MARY-CHAPIN CARPENTER
CAN'T STOP MYSELF ....PATTY LOVELESS
I WILL ALWAYS LOVE YOU ....DOLLY PARTON
SOME KIND OF TROUBLE ....TANYA TUCKER
ONE TIME AROUND ....MICHELLE WRIGHT
WRONG SIDE OF MEMPHIS ....TRISHA YEARWOOD

COUNTRY GUYS — CD1093
IF I DIDN'T HAVE YOU ....RANDY TRAVIS
WE SHALL BE FREE ....GARTH BROOKS
IF THERE HADN'T BEEN YOU ....BILLY DEAN
I CROSS MY HEART ....GEORGE STRAIT
WARNING LABELS ....DOUG STONE
COULD'VE BEEN ME ....BILLY RAY CYRUS
BOOT SCOOTIN' BOOGIE ....BROOKS & DUNN
RUNNIN' BEHIND ....TRACY LAWRENCE
I'LL THINK OF SOMETHING ....MARK CHESNUTT
THIS ONE'S GONNA HURT YOU ......M. STUART/T. TRITT

GUYS AND GALS - COUNTRY KARAOKE — CD1094
ROCK ME (IN THE CRADLE OF LOVE) ...DEBORAH ALLEN
TELL ME WHY ....WYNONNA
STANDING KNEE DEEP IN A RIVER ......KATHY MATTEA
THE CHANGE ....MICHELLE WRIGHT
YOU AND I ....RABBITT/GAYLE
AIN'T THAT LONELY YET ....DWIGHT YOAKAM
JUST AS I AM ....RICKY VAN SHELTON
LEARNING TO LIVE AGAIN ....GARTH BROOKS
SHE'S NOT CRYIN' ANYMORE ....BILLY RAY CYRUS

COUNTRY KARAOKE FOR WOMEN — CD1095
.YOU SAY YOU WILL ....
.........................TRISHA YEARWOOD
HEARTACHE ....SUZY BOGGUSS
THE HEART WON'T LIE .MCENTIRE/GILL
CONSTANT CRAVING ......K.D. LANG
MY STRONGEST WEAKNESS ...
...............................WYNONNA
ROMEO ....DOLLY PARTON
TAKE IT LIKE A MAN ...
.........................MICHELLE WRIGHT
LIFE HOLDS ON ......BETH N
CHAPMAN
THE TIME HAS COME ....MARTINA MCBRIDE
I GUESS YOU HAD TO BE THERE ......LORRIE MORGAN

MALE HITS OF THE 90'S — CD1096
THE CRYING GAME ...
.............BOY GEORGE
REACH OUT, I'LL BE THERE
......MICHAEL BOLTON
DO IT TO ME ...
.........LIONEL RICHIE
HEAL THE WORLD * .....
.....MICHAEL JACKSON
THE ONE ...ELTON JOHN
EVERY LITTLE STEP ....
.........BOBBY BROWN
IF EVER YOU'RE IN MY ARMS AGAIN ....
PEABO BRYSON
TOO FUNKY ....GEORGE MICHAEL
JUST ANOTHER DAY ....JON SECADA

HOT CHART HITS FOR WOMEN — CD1097
SAVING FOREVER FOR YOU ....SHANICE
SAVE THE BEST FOR LAST ....VANESSA WILLIAMS
DEEPER AND DEEPER ....MADONNA
REAL LOVE ....MARY J. BLIGE
SOMETIMES LOVE JUST AIN'T ENOUGH ....PATTY SMYTH
I'LL BE THERE ....MARIAH CAREY
WEAK ....SWV
THAT'S THE WAY LOVE GOES ....JANET JACKSON

FLAVORS OF ITALY — CD1098
MAMMA • TU CHE M'HAI PRESO IL CUOR • LA STRADA NEL BOSCO • UN AMORE COSI GRANDE • PARLA PIU PIANO • SANTA LUCIA • AL DI LA • CIAO BAMBINA • CUMME • NON TI SCORDAR DI ME • ITALIA

ITALIAN WEDDING — CD1099
TARANTELLA • SANTA LUCIA • AL DI LA • THAT'S AMORE (MEDLEY: #2 OF 2) • MAMMA • AH! MARIE • COME PRIMA • VOLARE (NEL BLU DIPINTO DI BLU) • SPEAK SOFTLY LOVE • TORNA A SURRIENTO (COME BACK TO SORRENTO) • O SOLE MIO • SUMMERTIME IN VENICE • ARRIVEDERCI ROMA (MEDLEY: #3 OF 3) • ANEMA E CORE • MALA FEMMENA (MEDLEY: #1 OF 3)

HITS OF REBA MCENTIRE, VOL.2 — CD1101
YOU LIE • FANCY • WALK ON • RUMOR HAS IT • FOR MY BROKEN HEART • THEY ASKED ABOUT YOU • IS THERE LIFE OUT THERE?* • LOVE WILL FIND IT'S WAY TO YOU • THE GREATEST MAN I NEVER KNEW • DOES HE LOVE YOU?

RHYTHM COUNTRY & BLUES — CD1102
SINCE I FELL FOR YOU ....R. MCENTIRE/N. COLE,
RAINY NIGHT IN GEORGIA ....C. TWITTY/S. MOORE
SOUTHERN NIGHTS ....C. ATKINS A.TOUSSAINT
WHEN SOMETHING IS WRONG W/MY BABY ....
.................................T. TRITT/P. LABELLE
FUNNY HOW TIME SLIPS AWAY ......L. LOVETT/A. GREEN
CHAIN OF FOOLS ....C. BLACK /POINTER SISTER
AIN'T NOTHING LIKE THE REAL THING .. V. GILL/G. KNIGHT
SOMETHIN' ELSE ....T. TUCKER/LITTLE RICHARD
I FALL TO PIECES ....T.YEARWOOD/ A. NEVILLE

HITS OF REBA MCENTIRE VOL.3 — CD1103
IT'S NOT OVER (IF I'M NOT OVER YOU) • I'M NOT THAT LONELY YET • IT'S YOUR CALL • FALLIN' OUT OF LOVE • HOW BLUE • I'M IN LOVE ALL OVER • CATHY'S CLOWN • MIND YOUR OWN BUSINESS • NEW FOOL AT AN OLD GAME* • ONLY IN MY MIND

LUSH BIG BAND SOUNDS — CD1104
YOU'RE DRIVING ME CRAZY • IT'S A SIN TO TELL A LIE • YOU MAKE ME FEEL SO YOUNG • FOOLS RUSH IN • EVERYWHERE YOU GO • MY BABY JUST CARES FOR ME • DAY IN, DAY OUT • NEAR YOU • DARN THAT DREAM • LITTLE WHITE LIES

SHOWSTOPPERS — CD1105
WHAT KIND OF FOOL AM I ....ANTHONY NEWLEY
NEW YORK, NEW YORK ....FRANK SINATRA
YOU'VE LOST THAT LOVIN' FEELIN ....RIGHTEOUS BROS.
YOU'LL NEVER FIND ANOTHER LOVE ....LOU RAWLS
THAT'S AMORE ....DEAN MARTIN
MONA LISA ....NAT COLE
OH, PRETTY WOMAN ...
.....................ROY ORBISON
A KISS TO BUILD A DREAM
ON ...LOUIS ARMSTRONG
IT HAD TO BE YOU ....
........HARRY CONNICK
I LEFT MY HEART IN SAN
FRANCISCO ...
.......TONY BENNETT

THE HAPPIEST MAN IN COUNTRY — CD1106
• WHAT SHE'S DOING NOW • THAT SUMMER • STANDING OUTSIDE THE FIRE • CALLIN' BATON ROUGE • AMERICAN HONKY-TONK BAR ASSOCIATION • AIN'T GOIN' DOWN ('TIL THE SUN COMES UP) • THE COWBOY SONG • THE NIGHT WILL ONLY KNOW • KICKIN' AND SCREAMIN' • ONE NIGHT A DAY

HITS OF MICHAEL BOLTON VOL.2 — CD1107
SOUL OF MY SOUL • SAID I LOVED YOU...BUT I LIED • THE ONE THING • A TIME FOR LETTING GO • IN THE ARMS OF LOVE • GEORGIA ON MY MIND • WHEN I'M BACK ON MY FEET AGAIN • HOW CAN WE BE LOVERS

PROFILE OF THE 80'S — CD1108
LADY ....KENNY ROGERS
PHYSICAL ....OLIVIA NEWTON-JOHN
EBONY AND IVORY ....MCCARTNEY/WONDER
EVERY BREATH YOU TAKE ....POLICE
LIKE A VIRGIN ....MADONNA
SAY YOU, SAY ME ....LIONEL RICHIE
ONE MORE TRY ....GEORGE MICHAEL
WALK LIKE AN EGYPTIAN ....THE BANGLES
ANOTHER DAY IN PARADISE* ....PHIL COLLINS

HITS OF REGGAE — CD1109
I SHOT THE SHERIFF .BOB MARLEY
NO WOMAN NO CRY . . . . .BOB MARLEY
COULD YOU BE LOVED . . . . .BOB MARLEY
THREE LITTLE BIRDS . . . . .BOB MARLEY
CAN'T HELP FALLING IN LOVE UB40
THE WAY YOU DO THE THINGS YOU DO UB40
LOOK WHO'S DANCIN' . . . . .ZIGGY MARLEY
ONE BRIGHT DAY . . . . .ZIGGY MARLEY

D.J. PARTY VOL.2 — CD1111
Y.M.C.A* . . . . .VILLAGE PEOPLE
THE SHOOP SHOOP SONG (IT'S IN HIS KISS)... .
NA NA HEY HEY (KISS HIM GOODBYE) . . . .
. . . . .THE STEAM
PIANO MAN . . . . .BILLY JOEL
THE TIME WARP . . . .(ROCKY HORROR SHOW)
GET ON YOUR FEET* . . . . .GLORIA ESTEFAN
KOKOMO .THE BEACH BOYS
LOUIE LOUIE . . . . .THE KINGSMEN
PINK CADILLAC* . . . . .NATALIE COLE
HANKY PANKY . . . . .TOMMY JAMES & SHONDELLS

D.J. PARTY VOL.3 — CD1112
OLD TIME ROCK AND ROLL . . . . .BOB SEGER
THAT'S THE WAY I LIKE IT .KC AND THE SUNSHINE BAND
ROCK THIS TOWN . . . . .STRAY CATS
I LOVE ROCK 'N' ROLL . . . . .JOAN JETT
LAST DANCE . . . . .DONNA SUMMER
WE DIDN'T START THE FIRE . . . . .BILLY JOEL
SMOKIN' IN THE BOYS' ROOM* . . . . .MOTLEY CRUE
JOHNNY B. GOODE . . . . .CHUCK BERRY
MONY, MONY . . . . .TOMMY JAMES & SHONDELLS
1-2-3* . . . . .MIAMI SOUND MACHINE

D.J. PARTY VOL.4 — CD1113
BORN TO BE WILD . . . . .STEPPENWOLF
MACHO MAN* . . . . .VILLAGE PEOPLE
SUPER FREAK .RICK JAMES
BAD TO THE BONE . . . . .GEORGE THOROGOOD
BAD GIRLS . . . . .DONNA SUMMER
SHORT PEOPLE . . . . .RANDY NEWMAN
DO YA THINK I'M SEXY . . . . .ROD STEWART
CARIBBEAN QUEEN . . . . .BILLY OCEAN
THE MONSTER MASH * . . . . .BOBBY PICKETT

THE COUNTRY COLLECTION — CD1114
LIVE UNTIL I DIE . . . . .CLAY WALKER
TRYIN' TO GET OVER YOU . . . . .VINCE GILL
WHAT MIGHT HAVE BEEN . . . . .LITTLE TEXAS
A LITTLE LESS TALK & A LOT MORE ACTION .TOBY KEITH
I WANT TO BE LOVED LIKE THAT . . . . .SHENANDOAH
THANK GOD FOR YOU . . . . .SAWYER BROWN
CAN'T BREAK IT TO MY HEART . . . . . . .TRACY LAWRENCE
HERE'S A QUARTER . . . . .TRAVIS TRITT
CHATTAHOOCHEE . . . . .ALAN JACKSON
IT SURE IS MONDAY . . . . .MARK CHESNUTT

PROP ME UP BESIDE THE JUKEBOX CD1115
AMERICAN BOY . . . . .EDDIE RABBITT
I'D LIKE TO HAVE THAT ONE BACK . . . . . .GEORGE STRAIT
HARD WORKIN' MAN . . . . .BROOKS & DUNN
HOMETOWN HONEYMOON . . . . .ALABAMA
PROP ME UP BESIDE THE JUKEBOX . . . . .JOE DIFFIE
AMERICAN HONKY-TONK BAR ASSOCIATION .G. BROOKS
I SWEAR . . . . .JOHN MICHAEL MONTGOMERY
ONE MORE LAST CHANCE . . . . .VINCE GILL
WHY DIDN'T I THINK OF THAT . . . . .DOUG STONE
WORKING MAN'S Ph.D. . . . . .AARON TIPPIN

COUNTRY'S BEST WOMEN — CD1116
MY STRONGEST WEAKNESS . . . . .WYNONNA
HEY CINDERELLA . . . . .SUZY BOGGUSS
HE THINKS HE'LL KEEP HER . .MARY CHAPIN CARPENTER
LIFE #9 . . . . .MARTINA MCBRIDE
LYING TO THE MOON . . . . .TRISHA YEARWOOD
HOW CAN I HELP YOU SAY GOODBYE . .PATTY LOVELESS
IT'S A LITTLE TOO LATE . . . . .TANYA TUCKER
I LOVE YOU 'CAUSE I WANT TO . . . . . .CARLENE CARTER
HEART TROUBLE . . . . .MARTINA MCBRIDE
WILD ONE . . . . .FAITH HILL

YOU SING THE SONGS OF
SINATRA

HITS OF FRANK SINATRA — CD1001
THE LADY IS A TRAMP • I'VE GOT YOU UNDER MY SKIN •
NIGHT AND DAY • I'VE GOT THE WORLD ON A STRING •
SUMMER WIND • WITCHCRAFT • STRANGERS IN THE NIGHT •
CHICAGO (THAT TODDLING TOWN) • MY WAY (COMME
D'HABITUDE) • NEW YORK, NEW YORK

BOBBY DARIN & FRANK SINATRA — CD1029
YOUNG AT HEART • HOW LITTLE WE KNOW • FOR ONCE IN
MY LIFE • COME FLY WITH ME • NICE 'N' EASYTHAT'S ALL •
CLEMENTINE • DREAM LOVER • BEYOND THE SEA • MACK
THE KNIFE

HITS OF FRANK SINATRA, VOL.3 — CD1050
FLY ME TO THE MOON • I WISH I WERE IN LOVE AGAIN • IT
STARTED ALL OVER AGAIN • LET'S FALL IN LOVE • LOVE AND
MARRIAGE • LOVE WALKED IN* • SATURDAY NIGHT (IS THE
LONELIEST NIGHT OF THE WEEK) • HIGH HOPES • ANYTHING
GOES • SHE'S FUNNY THAT WAY

HITS OF FRANK SINATRA, VOL.4 — CD1051
ALL OF ME • SERENADE IN BLUE • I'LL NEVER SMILE AGAIN •
LEARNIN' THE BLUES • THE TENDER TRAP (LOVE IS) • THE
SONG IS YOU • THEY CAN'T TAKE THAT AWAY FROM ME • I'LL
BE SEEING YOU • ALL OR NOTHING AT ALL • THIS LOVE OF
MINE

HITS OF FRANK SINATRA, VOL.5 — CD1075
SATISFY ME ONE MORE TIME • HOW DO YOU KEEP THE
MUSIC PLAYING? • TEACH ME TONIGHT • UNTIL THE REAL
THING COMES ALONG • IF I SHOULD LOSE YOU • THE BEST IS
YET TO COME • LUCK BE A LADY • I CONCENTRATE ON YOU •
THE COFFEE SONG • IT WAS A VERY GOOD YEAR

HITS OF FRANK SINATRA, VOL.6 — CD1082
IT'S ALL RIGHT WITH ME • YOU'D BE SO EASY TO LOVE •
HERE'S TO THE LOSERS • HEY, JEALOUS LOVER • DREAM •
ALL THE WAY • PENNIES FROM HEAVEN • CLOSE TO YOU •
YOUNG AT HEART • (LOVE IS) THE TENDER TRAP

SINATRA DUETS — CD1164
THE LADY IS A TRAMP • SUMMER WIND • NEW YORK, NEW
YORK • I'VE GOT A CRUSH ON YOU • I'VE GOT YOU UNDER
MY SKIN • WHAT NOW MY LOVE • COME RAIN OR COME
SHINE • THEY CAN'T TAKE THAT AWAY FROM ME • I'VE GOT
THE WORLD ON A STRING • WITCHCRAFT

SING SINATRA WITH STRINGS — CD1199
I HADN'T ANYONE TILL YOU • NIGHT AND DAY • MISTY •
STARDUST • COME RAIN OR COME SHINE • IT MIGHT AS
WELL BE SPRING • PRISONER OF LOVE • THAT'S ALL • ALL OR
NOTHING AT ALL • YESTERDAYS

WEE SMALL HOURS (SINATRA) — CD1192
I SEE YOUR FACE BEFORE ME • I'LL NEVER BE THE SAME •
THIS LOVE OF MINE • I GET ALONG WITHOUT YOU VERY
WELL • CAN'T WE BE FRIENDS • WHEN YOUR LOVER HAS
GONE • IN THE WEE SMALL HOURS • DANCING ON THE
CEILING • IT NEVER ENTERED MY MIND • I'LL BE AROUND

SOME STORY SONGS — CD1117
SOON . . . . .TANYA TUCKER
PIECE OF MY HEART . . . . .FAITH HILL
PASSIONATE KISSES . . . .
. . . . .MARY-CHAPIN CARPENTER
WHAT PART OF NO? . . . . .LORRIE MORGAN
THAT WASN'T ME . . . . . . .MARTINA MCBRIDE
THE SONG REMEMBERS WHEN . . . .
. . . . .TRISHA YEARWOOD
YOU JUST WATCH ME . . . . .TANYA TUCKER
ONLY LOVE . . . . .WYNONNA
DANCE WITH THE ONE . . . . .SHANIA TWAIN
ROCK BOTTOM . . . . .WYNONNA

MOTOWN MEMORIES (MALE) — CD1118
MY CHERIE AMOUR . . . . .STEVIE WONDER
I HEARD IT THROUGH THE GRAPEVINE . . .MARVIN GAYE
BABY, I NEED YOUR LOVING . . . . .FOUR TOPS
I CAN'T HELP MYSELF . . . . .FOUR TOPS
BEING WITH YOU . . . . .SMOKEY ROBINSON
HOW SWEET IT IS (TO BE LOVED BY YOU) MARVIN GAYE
I'LL BE THERE .JACKSON FIVE
MY GIRL . . . . .TEMPTATIONS
I SECOND THAT EMOTION . . . . .SMOKEY ROBINSON
YOU ARE THE SUNSHINE OF MY LIFE . .STEVIE WONDER

MOTOWN MEMORIES (FEMALE) — CD1119
STOP IN THE NAME OF LOVE . . . . .THE SUPREMES
PLEASE MR. POSTMAN . . . . .MARVELETTES
LOVE IS LIKE A HEATWAVE .MARTHA & THE VANDELLAS
MY GUY . . . . .MARY WELLS
WHERE DID OUR LOVE GO . . . . .THE SUPREMES
BABY LOVE . . . . .THE SUPREMES
DANCING IN THE STREET . .MARTHA & THE VANDELLAS
AIN'T NO MOUNTAIN HIGH ENOUGH . . . . .DIANA ROSS
IF I WERE YOUR WOMAN . . . . . . .GLADYS KNIGHT/PIPS
TOUCH ME IN THE MORNING . . . . .DIANA ROSS

HITS OF STEVIE WONDER — CD1120
BOOGIE ON REGGAE WOMAN • I JUST CALLED TO SAY I
LOVE YOU • ISN'T SHE LOVELY • HIGHER GROUND • YOU
AND I • SIR DUKE • FOR ONCE IN MY LIFE • RIBBON IN
THE SKY • SUPERSTITION • DO I DO

MEMORABLE MOVIE MUSIC — CD1122
BEAUTY AND THE BEAST* . . . . .DION/BRYSON
CABARET . . . . .LIZA MINELLI
WIND BENEATH MY WINGS . . . . .BETTE MIDLER
AS LONG AS HE NEEDS ME . . . .(OLIVER)
MY GUY (MY GOD) . . . .(SISTER ACT)
SHOUT! . . . .(SISTER ACT)
WHEN I FALL IN LOVE . . . . .CELINE DION/C. GRIFFIN
WHAT A WONDERFUL WORLD* . . .LOUIS ARMSTRONG,
I WILL ALWAYS LOVE YOU . . . . .WHITNEY HOUSTON
HELLO DOLLY . . . . .BARBRA STREISAND

COUNTRY CHRISTMAS — CD1123
BLUE CHRISTMAS . . . . .ELVIS PRESLEY
I BELIEVE IN SANTA CLAUS . . . . .ROGERS/PARTON
HARD CANDY CHRISTMAS . . . . .DOLLY PARTON
I'LL BE HOME FOR CHRISTMAS . . . . .AMY GRANT
WHITE CHRISTMAS . . . . .GARTH BROOKS
WINTER WONDERLAND . . . . .TRAVIS TRITT
CHRISTMAS WITHOUT YOU . . . . .ROGERS/PARTON
PRETTY PAPER . . . . .WILLIE NELSON
CHRISTMAS IN DIXIE . . . . .ALABAMA
THE GREATEST GIFT OF ALL . . . . .ROGERS/PARTON
WITH BELLS ON . . . . .ROGERS/PARTON

HAPPY SONGS ARE HERE AGAIN — CD1124
SOMEBODY STOLE MY GAL (MEDLEY) • YES SIR, THAT'S
MY BAB (MEDLEY) • OH, YOU BEAUTIFUL DOLL
(MEDLEY) • THAT OLD GANG OF MINE (MEDLEY)
MELANCHOLY BABY (MEDLEY) • PEG O' MY HEART
(MEDLEY) • BYE BYE BLUES (MEDLEY) • I'LL SEE YOU IN
MY DREAMS (MEDLEY) • GOODNIGHT SWEETHEART
(MEDLEY) • HAPPY DAYS ARE HERE AGAIN (MEDLEY) •
I'M SITTING ON TOP OF THE WORLD (MEDLEY) • I'M
LOOKING OVER A FOUR LEAF CLOVER (MEDLEY) • HAIL,
HAIL THE GANG'S ALL HERE (MEDLEY) • ALABAMA
JUBILEE (MEDLEY) • BABY FACE (MEDLEY) • I WANT TO
BE HAPPY (MEDLEY) • BYE BYE BLACKBIRD (MEDLEY) •
ME AND MY SHADOW (MEDLEY) • MOONLIGHT AND
ROSES (MEDLEY) • YOU WERE MEANT FOR ME
(MEDLEY) • YOU ARE MY SUNSHINE (MEDLEY) • HAPPY
SONGS ARE HERE AGAIN

OLD SONGS ARE THE BEST SONGS
CD1125
MARGIE (MEDLEY) • PUT YOUR ARMS AROUND ME, HONEY (MEDLEY) • MA, HE'S MAKIN' EYES AT ME (MEDLEY) • THE BAND PLAYED ON (MEDLEY) • SWEET GEORGIA BROWN (MEDLEY) • PENNIES FROM HEAVEN (MEDLEY) • ON THE SUNNY SIDE OF THE STREET (MEDLEY) • THE SIDEWALKS OF NEW YORK (MEDLEY) • WHEN THE RED, RED ROBIN COMES BOB, BOB BOBBIN' ALONG (MEDLEY) • TAKE ME OUT TO THE BALL GAME (MEDLEY) • SIDE BY SIDE (MEDLEY) • MY BLUE HEAVEN (MEDLEY) • IN A SHANTY IN OLD SHANTY TOWN (MEDLEY) • ALEXANDER'S RAGTIME BAND (MEDLEY) • HEART OF MY HEART (MEDLEY) • GIVE MY REGARDS TO BROADWAY • HELLO DOLLY

BRILL BUILDING - NEIL DIAMOND   CD1126
DO YOU KNOW THE WAY TO SAN JOSE • DON'T MAKE ME OVER • DON'T BE CRUEL (TO A HEART THAT'S TRUE) • YOU'VE LOST THAT LOVIN' FEELIN' • I (WHO HAVE NOTH-ING)* • A GROOVY KIND OF LOVE • SPANISH HARLEM* • SAVE THE LAST DANCE FOR ME • HAPPY BIRTHDAY, SWEET SIXTEEN • WILL YOU STILL LOVE ME TOMORROW

ELTON JOHN DUETS   CD1128
WHEN I THINK ABOUT LOVE • THE POWER • SHAKEY GROUND • DON'T GO BREAKING MY HEART • DON'T LET THE SUN GO DOWN ON ME • GO ON AND ON • AIN'T NOTHING LIKE THE REAL THING • LOVE LETTERS

HITS OF TONY BENNETT   CD1129
NICE WORK IF YOU CAN GET IT • CHANGE PARTNERS • ONE FOR MY BABY (AND ONE MORE FOR THE ROAD) • IT ONLY HAPPENS WHEN I DANCE WITH YOU • THE BOULEVARD OF BROKEN DREAMS • EMILY • BODY AND SOUL • SPEAK LOW • THE DAYS OF WINE AND ROSES • STEPPIN' OUT WITH MY BABY

HITS OF TONY BENNETT VOL.2   CD1131
THEY SAY IT'S WONDERFUL • BECAUSE OF YOU • GIRL TALK • I'LL BE SEEING YOU • THE FOLKS WHO LIVE ON THE HILL • TIME AFTER TIME • WHY DO PEOPLE FALL IN LOVE? • LET'S FACE THE MUSIC AND DANCE • DANCING IN THE DARK • ALL OF YOU

HITS OF MARIAH CAREY   CD1132
DREAMLOVER* • HERO* • ANYTIME YOU NEED A FRIEND* • JUST TO HOLD YOU ONCE AGAIN* • WITHOUT YOU • SOMEDAY* • LOVE TAKES TIME* • MAKE IT HAPPEN* • VISION OF LOVE*

OLDIES PARTY VOL.1   CD1135
WOOLY BULLY . . . . .SAM THE SHAM
Y.M.C.A * . . . . .VILLAGE PEOPLE
BAD MOON RISING . . . . . . .CREEDENCE CLEARWATER REV
OH, PRETTY WOMAN . . . . .ROY ORBISON,
MONDAY, MONDAY . . . . .MAMAS AND THE PAPAS
THE WANDERER . . . . .DION AND THE BELMONTS
BLUEBERRY HILL . . . . .FATS DOMINO
DA DOO RON RON * . . . . .THE CRYSTALS
BYE BYE LOVE . . . . .THE EVERLY BROTHERS
NIGHTS IN WHITE SATIN . . . . .THE MOODY BLUES

OLDIES PARTY VOL.2   CD1136
LA BAMBA . . . . .RICHIE VALENS
CHARLIE BROWN . . . . .THE COASTERS
CALIFORNIA GIRLS . . . . . . .THE BEACH BOYS
MACK THE KNIFE . . . . .BOBBY DARIN
HAPPY TOGETHER . . . . .TURTLES
THE LION SLEEPS TONIGHT . . . . .TOKENS
MR. TAMBOURINE MAN * . . . . .BYRDS
DO WAH DIDDY DIDDY . . . . .MANFRED MANN
THE LETTER . . . . .BOX TOPS
MRS. ROBINSON * . . . . . SIMON AND GARFUNKEL

HITS OF THE BEATLES VOL.2
CD1137
I WANT TO HOLD YOUR HAND • NOWHERE MAN • AND I LOVE HER • GOOD DAY SUNSHINE • HELP! • YELLOW SUBMARINE • SHE LOVES YOU • BLACKBIRD • ALL MY LOVING • I FEEL FINE

HITS OF THE BEATLES VOL.3   CD1138
GOT TO GET YOU INTO MY LIFE • LADY MADONNA • DO YOU WANT TO KNOW A SECRET • ALL YOU NEED IS LOVE • WHILE MY GUITAR GENTLY WEEPS • SOMETHING • YOU'VE GOT TO HIDE YOUR LOVE AWAY • ACROSS THE UNIVERSE • DRIVE MY CAR • LONG AND WINDING ROAD

HITS OF THE BEATLES VOL.4   CD1139
I SAW HER STANDING THERE • BACK IN THE U.S.S.R. • P.S. I LOVE YOU • LUCY IN THE SKY WITH DIAMONDS • TICKET TO RIDE • PLEASE, PLEASE ME • CAN'T BUY ME LOVE • IN MY LIFE • MAXWELL'S SILVER HAMMER • GET BACK

HITS OF THE BEATLES VOL.5   CD1140
SGT.PEPPER'S LONELY HEARTS CLUB BAND • DAY TRIPPER • HERE, THERE AND EVERYWHERE • OB-LA-DI, OB-LA-DA • LOVE ME DO • WHEN I'M SIXTY-FOUR • TWIST AND SHOUT • WITH A LITTLE HELP FROM MY FRIENDS • HERE COMES THE SUN • A HARD DAY'S NIGHT

HITS OF THE BEATLES VOL.6   CD1141
WE CAN WORK IT OUT • EIGHT DAYS A WEEK • IF I FELL • A DAY IN THE LIFE • COME TOGETHER • PAPERBACK WRITER • FROM ME TO YOU • REVOLUTION • SHE'S A WOMAN •FIXING A HOLE

JULIO IGLESIAS EN ESPANOL   CD1142
ABRAZAME • POR UN POCO DE TU AMOR • A VECES TU, A VECES YO • POR EL AMOR DE UNA MUJER • ME OLVIDE DE VIVIR • EL AMOR • MANUELA • 33 ANOS • Y AUNQUE TE HAGA CALOR • SOMOS

THE BIG CHILL ERA   CD1143
STAND BY ME . . . . .BEN E. KING
LOUIE LOUIE . . . . .THE KINGSMEN
YOU'VE REALLY GOT A HOLD ON ME SMOKEY ROBINSON
(SITTIN' ON) THE DOCK OF THE BAY . . . . . .OTIS REDDING
BLUE VELVET . . . . .BOBBY VINTON
I HEARD IT THROUGH THE GRAPEVINE . . . . .MARVIN GAYE
LET'S TWIST AGAIN . . . . .CHUBBY CHECKER
SHOUT! . . . . .ISLEY BROTHERS
MY GIRL . . . . .TEMPTATIONS
BABY, I NEED YOUR LOVING . . . . .FOUR TOPS

BIG BAND CLASSICS VOL.1   CD1145
A KISS TO BUILD A DREAM ON . . . . . .LOUIS ARMSTRONG
I'VE HEARD THAT SONG BEFORE . . . . .HARRY JAMES
I HAD THE CRAZIEST DREAM . . . . .HARRY JAMES
IT'S BEEN A LONG, LONG TIME . . . . .HARRY JAMES
CHATTANOOGA CHOO-CHOO . . . . .GLENN MILLER
SERENADE IN BLUE . . . . .GLENN MILLER
DON'T SIT UNDER THE APPLE TREE . . . . . .GLENN MILLER
TANGERINE . . . . .JIMMY DORSEY
I UNDERSTAND . . . . .JIMMY DORSEY
ALL OR NOTHING AT ALL . . . . .JIMMY DORSEY

BIG BAND CLASSICS VOL.2   CD1146
I CRIED FOR YOU .HARRY JAMES
YOU MADE ME LOVE YOU . . . . .HARRY JAMES
ELMER'S TUNE . . . . .GLENN MILLER
NIGHTINGALE SANG, A * . . . . .GLENN MILLER
AT LAST . . . . .GLENN MILLER
BRAZIL . . . . .JIMMY DORSEY
MARIA ELENA . . . . .JIMMY DORSEY
YOURS . . . . .JIMMY DORSEY
CABARET . . . . .LOUIS ARMSTRONG
WHAT A WONDERFUL WORLD * . . . . .LOUIS ARMSTRONG

MEET THE FLINTSTONES   CD1147
MEET THE FLINTSTONES . . . . .THE BC-52's
ROCK WITH THE CAVEMAN . . . . .BIG AUDIO DYNAMITE
I SHOWED A CAVEMAN . . . . .US3 FEATURING DEF JEF
WALK THE DINOSAUR . . . . .WAS NOT WAS
BEDROCK ANTHEM * . . . . .WEIRD AL YANKOVIC
I WANNA BE A FLINTSTONE .SCREAMING BLUE MESSIAHS
IN THE DAYS OF THE CAVEMAN . . .CRASH TEST DUMMIES
HUMAN BEING (BEDROCK STEADY) . . . . . . .STEREO MC'S
HIT & RUN HOLIDAY . . . . .MY LIFE WITH THE T.K.K.
THE BEDROCK TWITCH . . . . .THE BC-52's

THE WAY HE MAKES ME FEEL   CD1148
THE WAY HE MAKES ME FEEL • GUILTY • WHAT KIND OF FOOL • WOMAN IN LOVE • MY HEART BELONGS TO ME • PAPA, CAN YOU HEAR ME? • BEING ALIVE • NOT WHILE I'M AROUND • A PIECE OF SKY • ORDINARY MIRACLES

FEMALE LATIN HITS   CD1149
AYER* . . . . .GLORIA ESTEFAN
LA LLAMADA . . . . .SELENA
UN CORAZON HECHO PEDAZOS . . . . . . .EDNITA NAZARIO
VELETA . . . . .LUCERO
SE ME OLVIDO OTRA VEZ . . . . . . .YOLANDA DEL RIO
CON LOS ANOS QUE ME QUEDAN * . . .GLORIA ESTEFAN
MIRALA MIRALO . . . . .ALEJANDRA GUZMAN
TRES DESEOS . . . . .EDNITA NAZARIO
NO DEBES JUGAR . . . . .SELENA

CONTEMPORARY MALE LATIN HITS   CD1150
TU Y YO . . . . .LUIS MIGUEL
CARA DE NINO . . . . .JERRY RIVERA
SENTIR . . . . .JON SECADA
SI NO SE ACABO TU AMOR . . . . .JOHNNY RIVERA
40 Y 20 . . . . .JOSE JOSE
SUAVE/MIGUEL, LUISELLA ES . . .FANTASMAS DEL CARIBE
SIEMPRE EN MI CORAZON . . . . .PLACIDO DOMINGO
QUIERO . . . . .JULIO IGLESIAS

JEKYLL & HYDE   CD1151
THIS IS THE MOMENT • LOVE HAS COME OF AGE • ONCE UPON A DREAM (FEMALE) • SOMEONE LIKE YOU • TILL YOU CAME INTO MY LIFE • NO ONE KNOWS WHO I AM • A NEW LIFE • ONCE UPON A DREAM (MALE)

HITS OF BON JOVI   CD1152
BED OF ROSES • BLAZE OF GLORY • I'LL BE THERE FOR YOU • NEVER SAY GOODBYE • RUNAWAY • YOU GIVE LOVE A BAD NAME • SILENT NIGHT • BAD MEDICINE

COUNTRY OLDIES - MALE   CD1153
THE MOST BEAUTIFUL GIRL . . . . .CHARLIE RICH
TAKE ME HOME, COUNTRY ROADS . . . . .JOHN DENVER
FOR THE GOOD TIMES . . . . .RAY PRICE
ALWAYS ON MY MIND . . . . .WILLIE NELSON
JAMBALAYA (ON THE BAYOU) . . . . .HANK WILLIAMS
SIX DAYS ON THE ROAD . . . . .DAVE DUDLEY
KING OF THE ROAD . . . . .ROGER MILLER
I WALK THE LINE .JOHNNY CASH
GREEN, GREEN GRASS OF HOME . . . . .TOM JONES
LUCILLE . . . . .KENNY ROGERS

COUNTRY OLDIES - FEMALE   CD1154
STAND BY YOUR MAN . . . . .TAMMY WYNETTE
ROSE GARDEN .LYNN ANDERSON
HARPER VALLEY P.T.A. . . . . .JEANNIE C. RILEY
ODE TO BILLY JOE . . . . .BOBBIE GENTRY
THESE BOOTS WERE MADE FOR WALKIN' NANCY SINATRA
NINE TO FIVE . . . . .DOLLY PARTON
JUST ANOTHER WOMAN IN LOVE . . . . . . .ANNE MURRAY
BLUE KENTUCKY GIRL . . . . .EMMYLOU HARRIS
DON'T IT MAKE MY BROWN EYES BLUE . .CRYSTAL GAYLE
SWEET DREAMS .PATSY CLINE

WOODSTOCK REVISITED
CD1155

PROUD MARY . . . . .TINA TURNER
WOODSTOCK . . . . .JONI MITCHELL
DANCE TO THE MUSIC* . . . . .SLY AND THE FAMILY STONE
SOMEBODY TO LOVE . . . . .JEFFERSON AIRPLANE
PIECE OF MY HEART . . . . .JANIS JOPLIN
EVIL WAYS . . . . .SANTANA
WITH A LITTLE HELP FROM MY FRIENDS . . . .JOE COCKER
WE'RE NOT GONNA TAKE IT * . . . . .THE WHO
THE NIGHT THEY DROVE OLD DIXIE DOWN . . . .JOAN BAEZ

LOVE DUETS
CD1156

TONIGHT I CELEBRATE . . . . .FLACK/BRYSON
ENDLESS LOVE . . . . .L. RICHIE/D. ROSS
WE DIDN'T KNOW . . . . .HOUSTON/WONDER
A WHOLE NEW WORLD* . . . . .BRYSON/BELLE
WHEN I FALL IN LOVE . . . . .C. DION/C. GRIFFIN
YOU'RE ALL I NEED TO GET BY . . . . .GAYE/TERRELL
THE BEST THINGS IN LIFE ARE FREE .VANDROSS/JACKSON
LOVE IS . . . . .MCKNIGHT/WILLIAMS
BABY, COME TO ME . . . . .AUSTIN/INGRAM

COUNTRY WEDDING
CD1157

YOU AND I . . . . .C. GAYLE & E. RABBITT
I SWEAR . . . . .JOHN MICHAEL MONTGOMERY
AT LAST . . . . .GENE WATSON
THAT'S ALL .KATHY LEE GIFFORD
ALL I HAVE . . . . .BETH NIELSEN CHAPMAN
I CROSS MY HEART . . . . .GEORGE STRAIT
VOWS GO UNBROKEN . . . . .KENNY ROGERS
PLEDGING MY LOVE . . . . .EMMYLOU HARRIS
THERE'S NO LOVE LIKE OUR LOVE .C. GAYLE & G. MORRIS
FOREVER AND EVER, AMEN . . . . .RANDY TRAVIS

COASTERS & THE DRIFTERS
CD1158

YAKETY YAK • CHARLIE BROWN • SEARCHIN' • POISON IVY •
YOUNG BLOOD • THERE GOES MY BABY • THIS MAGIC
MOMENT • ON BROADWAY • UP ON THE ROOF • SOME
KIND OF WONDERFUL

LOVE SONGS FOR A WEDDING
CD1159

UNCHAINED MELODY . . . . .RIGHTEOUS BROTHERS
CAN YOU FEEL THE LOVE TONIGHT * . . . . . . .ELTON JOHN
INSEPARABLE . . . . .NATALIE COLE
A WHOLE NEW WORLD* . . . . .BRYSON/BELLE
WHEN YOU TELL ME . . . . .J. IGLESIAS/D. PARTON
I WILL ALWAYS LOVE YOU . . . . .WHITNEY HOUSTON
ALL I HAVE . . . . .BETH NIELSEN CHAPMAN
BEAUTIFUL IN MY EYES . . . . .JOSHUA KADISON
TRUE COMPANION . . . . .MARC COHN

HITS OF CELINE DION
CD1161

THINK TWICE • MISLED • WHEN I FALL IN LOVE • IF YOU
ASKED ME TO • NOTHING BROKEN BUT MY HEART • LOVE
CAN MOVE MOUNTAINS • THE POWER OF LOVE • WHERE
DOES MY HEART BEAT NOW? • THE COLOUR OF MY LOVE

HITS OF ANITA BAKER VOL.2
CD1163

RHYTHM OF LOVE • BODY AND SOUL • SOUL INSPIRATION •
SWEET LOVE • YOU BELONG TO ME • SOMETIMES I
WONDER WHY • LOOK OF LOVE, THE • I APOLOGIZE

ELTON JOHN DUETS
CD1165

THE POWER • SHAKEY GROUND •
IF YOU WERE ME • DON'T GO BREAKING MY HEART •
DON'T LET THE SUN GO DOWN ON ME • TEARDROPS •
AIN'T NOTHING LIKE THE REAL THING • LOVE LETTERS

HITS OF STING
CD1166

IF I EVER LOSE MY FAITH IN YOU • WHEN WE DANCE •
NOTHING 'BOUT ME • FORTRESS AROUND YOUR HEART •
IF YOU LOVE SOMEBODY, SET THEM FREE • BE STILL MY
BEATING HEART • LOVE IS THE SEVENTH WAVE • RUSSIANS
• WE'LL BE TOGETHER

THE BEST OF R & B VOL. 1
CD1190

BABY, I NEED YOUR LOVING . . . . .FOUR TOPS
MY GIRL . . . . .TEMPTATIONS
UNDER THE BOARDWALK . . . . .DRIFTERS
WELL-A-WIGGY . . . . .WEATHER GIRLS
WHAT A WONDERFUL WORLD* . . . . .SAM COOKE,
RAINY DAY BELLS . . . . .GLOBETROTTERS
I KNOW I'M LOSING YOU . . . . .TEMPTATIONS
ANOTHER SATURDAY NIGHT* . . . . .SAM COOKE
I CAN'T HELP MYSELF . . . . .FOUR TOPS
UP ON THE ROOF . . . . .DRIFTERS

IN THE WEE SMALL HOURS
CD1192

I SEE YOUR FACE BEFORE ME • I'LL NEVER BE THE SAME •
THIS LOVE OF MINE • I GET ALONG WITHOUT YOU VERY
WELL • CAN'T WE BE FRIENDS • WHEN YOUR LOVER HAS
GONE • IN THE WEE SMALL HOURS • DANCING ON THE
CEILING • IT NEVER ENTERED MY MIND • I'LL BE AROUND

SING SONGS OF DISNEY
CD1198

COLORS OF THE WIND • CAN YOU FEEL THE LOVE
TONIGHT • CIRCLE OF LIFE • HAKUNA MATATA • I JUST
CAN'T WAIT TO BE KING • THE LION SLEEPS TONIGHT •
COLORS OF THE WIND • IF I NEVER KNEW YOU • JUST
AROUND THE RIVER BEND • BE OUR GUEST • BEAUTY AND
THE BEAST • A WHOLE NEW WORLD • UNDER THE SEA

THE SONGS BETTE MIDLER SINGS
CD1200

IN THIS LIFE • IT'S TOO LATE • I BELIEVE IN YOU • I KNOW
THIS TOWN • TO DESERVE YOU • THE PERFECT KISS •
BOTTOMLESS • TO COMFORT YOU • BED OF ROSES • AS
DREAMS GO BY • THE LAST TIME

YOU SING HOOTIE & THE BLOWFISH
CD1201

HOLD MY HAND • RUNNING FROM AN ANGEL • HANNAH
JANE • LET HER CRY • I'M GOIN' HOME • ONLY WANNA BE
WITH YOU • TIME • NOT EVEN THE TREES • DROWNING •
GOODBYE

YOU SING REGINA BELLE '95 HITS!
CD1202

COULD IT BE I'M FALLING IN LOVE • LOVE T.K.O. • YOU
MAKE ME FEEL BRAND NEW • HURRY UP THIS WAY AGAIN
• THE WHOLE TOWN'S LAUGHING AT ME • DIDN'T I (BLOW
YOUR MIND THIS TIME) • YOU ARE EVERYTHING • LET ME
MAKE LOVE TO YOU • JUST DON'T WANT TO BE LONELY •
I'LL BE AROUND

HITS OF ABBA
CD3001

THE FERNANDO • ANGEL EYES • DANCING QUEEN
• KNOWING ME, KNOWING YOU • SUPER TROUPER
• THE WINNER TAKES IT ALL • WATERLOO • TAKE A
CHANCE ON ME

HITS OF JOE COCKER
CD3002

UNCHAIN MY HEART • THE LETTER • CRY ME A RIVER • UP
WHERE WE BELONG • THE SIMPLE THINGS • HAVE A LITTLE
FAITH • TRUST IN ME (FROM • WITH A LITTLE HELP FROM
MY FRIENDS

HITS OF R.E.M.
CD3003

EVERYBODY HURTS • IT'S THE END OF THE WORLD AS WE
KNOW IT • LOSING MY RELIGION • THE ONE I LOVE • RADIO
FREE EUROPE • SHINY HAPPY PEOPLE • STAND • WHAT'S
THE FREQUENCY KENNETH

HITS OF PHIL COLLINS VOL. 2
CD3004

ANOTHER DAY IN PARADISE • DO YOU REMEMBER •
EVERYDAY • FIND A WAY TO MY HEART • I WISH IT WOULD
RAIN • ONLY YOU KNOW AND I KNOW • SOMETHING
HAPPENED ON THE WAY TO HEAVEN

HITS OF INXS
CD3005

BEAUTIFUL GIRL • DEVIL INSIDE • NEED YOU TONIGHT •
NEVER TEAR US APART • SUICIDE BLONDE • NEW
SENSATION • SHINING STAR • WHAT YOU NEED

HITS OF ERIC CLAPTON
CD3006

AFTER MIDNIGHT • I SHOT THE SHERIFF • LAYLA (MTV
UNPLUGGED) • I'M TORE DOWNLAY DOWN SALLY •
MOTHERLESS CHILD • TEARS IN HEAVEN • HOOCHIE
COOCHIE MAN

HITS OF BRYAN ADAMS
CD3008

CAN'T STOP THIS THING WE STARTED • DO I HAVE TO SAY
THE WORDS • PLEASE FORGIVE ME • SUMMER OF '69 •
THOUGHT I'D DIED AND GONE TO HEAVEN • ALL FOR LOVE
• (EVERYTHING I DO) I DO IT FOR YOU

HITS OF ROXETTE
CD3009

DANGEROUS • DRESSED FOR SUCCESS • IT MUST HAVE
BEEN LOVE • JOYRIDE • LOOK, THE • SLEEPING IN MY CAR
• FADING LIKE A FLOWER • LISTEN TO YOUR HEART •
CHURCH OF YOUR HEART

HITS OF THE ROLLING STONES
CD3010

START ME UP • HARLEM SHUFFLE • IT'S ONLY ROCK AND
ROLL • LOVE IS STRONG • YOU GOT ME ROCKING • OUT OF
TEARS • SATISFACTION • ANGIE

BROADWAY SHOWS TO GO!

Sugg. Retail Price: **$22.98** per Compact Disc; **$29.98** per 2 CD Set
$18.98 per Extended Play Cassette, which numbers are shown to the right of each listing
The greatest shows of the 20th Century, now available with and without vocals, to put you on-stage on Broadway.

CD 1197　SMOKEY JOE'S CAFE　PS2340
On Broadway • Poison Ivy • Charlie Brown • Stand by Me • Loving You • Hound Dog • There Goes My Baby • Jailhouse Rock • Spanish Harlem • Yakety Yak

CD 1196　GREASE　PS1505
Summer Nights • Rock 'N' Roll is Here to Stay • Sandy• Hopelessly Devoted to You • You're the One that I Want • Grease • Greased Lightnin' • Born to Hand Jive • We Go Together • Look at Me, I'm Sandra Dee • Those Magic Changes • There are Worse Things I Could Do • Blue Moon

CD 1193　SUNSET BOULEVARD　PS2262
Surrender • With One Look • The Greatest Star of All • Girl Meets Boy • New Ways to Dream • The Perfect Year • Sunset Boulevard • As if We Never Said Goodbye • Too Much in Love to Care

CD 1189　OLIVER (2 CD SET)　PS 89
• As Long As He Needs Me • Be Back Soon • Boy for Sale • Consider Yourself • Finale · Food, Glorious Food • I Shall Scream • I'd Do Anything It's A Fine Life • My name is Oliver! • Oom-Pah-Pah • Overture • Pick A Pocket Or Two • Reviewing The Situation • That's Your Funeral • Where Is Love? • Who Will Buy?

CD 1187　HELLO DOLLY (2 CD SET)　PS 87
• Before The Parade Passes By • Dancing • Elegance • Finale Ultimo • Hello Dolly • I Put My Hand In • It Only Takes A Moment • It Takes A Woman • Opening: Act 1 · Put On Your Sunday Clothes • Ribbons Down My Back • So Long Dearie

CD 1186 ANNIE GET YOUR GUN (2 CD's)PS 86
• Anything You Can Do • Colonel Buffalo Bill • Doin' What Comes Naturally • The Girl That I Marry • I Got Lost In His Arms • I Got The Sun In The Morning • I'm A Bad, Bad Man • I'm An Indian Too • Moonshine Lullaby • My Defenses Are Down • Old Fash-ioned Wedding • Overture • There's No Business Like Show Bus-iness • They Say It's Wonderful You Can't Get A Man With a Gun

CD 1184　SHOWBOAT　PS 84
• After The Ball • Bally-Hoo • Bill • Can't Help Lovin' Dat Man Of Mine • Finale - I Might Fall Back On You • Life Upon The Wicked stage • Make Believe • Ol' Man River • Opening: Cotton Blossom • Overture • Till Good Luck Comes My Way • Why Do I Love You • You Are Love

CD 1183　THE MUSIC MAN　PS 83
• Gary, Indiana • Good Night My Someone • If You Don't Mind My Saying So • Iowa Stubborn • Lida Rose/ Will I Ever Tell You • Marian The Librarian • My White Knight • Overture • Pick A Little,Talk A Little • The Sadder But Wiser Girl • Seventy-Six Trombones • Shipoopi • Sincere • Till There Was You • The Wells Fargo Wagon • Ya Got Trouble

CD 1181　PORGY AND BESS　PS 81
• Bess, Oh Where's My Bess • Bess, You Is My Woman Now • Gone, Gone, Gone • I Got Plenty Of Nuttin' • I Loves You Porgy • It Ain't Necessarily So • My Man's Gone Now • Oh I Can't Sit Down • Oh Lawd, I'm On My Way • Oh, Heavenly Father • Straw-berry Woman • Summertime • There's A Boat Dat's Leavin' Soon For New York • A Woman Is A Sometime Thing

CD 1180 CAROUSEL PS 80
• Blow High, Blow Low • The Carousel Waltz • The Highest Judge Of All • If I Loved You • June Is Bustin' Out all Over • Mister Snow • A Real Nice Clambake • Soliloquy • Stonecutters Cut It On Stone • What's The Use Of Wonderin' • When The Children are Asleep • You'll Never Walk Alone • You're A Queer One, Julie Jordan

CD 1179　FIDDLER ON THE ROOF　PS 79
• Anatevka • Do You Love Me? • Far From the Home I Love • If I Were a Rich Man • Matchmaker, Matchmaker • Miracles Of Miracles • Now I Have Everything • Sabbath Prayer • Sunrise, Sunset • Tevye's Dream • To Life • Tradition

CD 1178　THE KING AND I (2 CD SET)　PS 78
• Getting to Know You • Hello Young Lovers • I Have Dreamed • I Whistle a Happy Tune • March of The Siamese Children • My Lord And Master • Overture • A Puzzlement • Shall I Tell You What I Think of You • Shall We Dance • Something Wonderful • We Kiss in a Shadow

CD 1177　SOUTH PACIFIC　PS 77
• Bali Ha'i • Bloody Mary • A Cock-Eyed Optimist • Dites-Moi • Happy Talk • Honey Bun • I'm Gonna Wash That Man Right Outa My Hair • Overture • Some Enchanted Evening • There Is Nothin' Like A Dame • This Nearly Was Mine • Twin Soliloquies • A Wonderful Guy • You've Got To Be Carefully Taught • Younger Than Springtime

CD 1176　THE SOUND OF MUSIC　PS 76
• Canticle • Climb Every Mountain • Do Re Mi • Edelweiss • How Can Love Survive • The Lonely Goatherd • Maria • My Favorite Things • No Way to Stop It • An Ordinary Couple • Overture • Sixteen Going on Seventeen • So Long, Farewell • The Sound Of Music

CD 1175　OKLAHOMA　PS 75
• All 'Er Nothin' • The Farmer And The Cowman • I Can't Say No • Kansas City • Lonely Room • Many A New Day • Oh What A Beautiful Morning • Oklahoma • Out Of My Dreams • Overture • People Will Say We're In Love • Pore Jud Is Daid • The Surrey With The Fringe On Top.

CD 1174　MY FAIR LADY (2 CD set)　PS 74
• The Ascot Gavotte • Get Me To The Church On Time • A Hymn to Him • I Could Have Danced All Night • I'm An Ordinary Man • I've Grown Accustomed To Her Face • Just You Wait • On The Street Where You Live • Overture • The Rain In Spain • Show Me • Why Can't The English • With A Little Bit Of Luck • Without You • Wouldn't It Be Lovely • You Did It

CD 1173　CAMELOT　PS 73
• Before I Gaze At You Again • C'est Moi • Camelot • Follow Me • How To Handle A Woman • I Loved You Once In Silence • I Wonder What The King Is Doing Tonight • If Ever I Would Leave You • The Lusty Month Of May • Overture • The Simple Joys Of Maidenhood • What Do The Simple Folk Do.

CD 1054 HITS OF ANDREW LLOYD WEBBER　PS 842/843/844
• The Music of the Night • All I Ask of You • Memory • Seeing Is Believing • Love Changes Everything • Don't Cry for Me Argentina • I Don't Know How to Love Him • There's Me • Close Every Door
Printed lyrics not included at publisher's direction

CD 1151 JEKYLL & HYDE　PS 583
• Once Upon A Dream • Love Has Come of Age • This is the Moment • Someone Like You • Till You Came into My Life • No One Knows Who I Am • A New Life • Once Upon a Dream

CD 1144　BARBRA'S BROADWAY PS2209/2218
• Speak Low • With One Look • Luck Be a Lady • The Man I Love • Children Will Listen • Everybody Says Don't • The Music of the Night • Some Enchanted Evening • I've Never Been In Love Before

CD 1134　BROADWAY MELODIES　PS 373
• Try To Remember • Give My Regards to Broadway • Thank Heaven for Little Girls • I've Never Been in Love Before • It Only Takes a Moment • I Believe in You • This is the Moment • Shall We Dance • Stranger in Paradise • The Man I Love

CD 1133 THE SOUND OF BROADWAY　PS 601-617
• If I Were a Rich Man • I Could Have Danced All Night • Hello Dolly • Oh What a Beautiful Morning • On the Street Where You Live • Get Me to the Church on Time • Cabaret • What I Did for Love • Somewhere • Memory

CD 1130　BEST OF ANDREW LLOYD WEBER　PS 743/845
• Unexpected Song • Love Changes Everything • Seeing Is Believing • There Is More to Love • The First Man You Remember • Anything But Lonely • Angel of Music • Phantom of the Opera • Could We Start Again, Please? • Jesus Christ Superstar • Uncoupled
Printed lyrics not included at publisher's direction

CD 1110　CABARET (2 CD SET)　PS 1502
• Cabaret • Don't Tell Mama • If You Could See Her • It Couldn't Please Me More • Maybe This Time • Mein Herr • The Money Song • Perfectly Marvelous • Tomorrow Belongs To Me • Two Ladies • Why Should I Wake Up • Willkommen

CD 1100　WEST SIDE STORY (2 CD)　PS1501
• America • A Boy Like That • Cool • The Dance At The Gym • Finale • Gee Officer Krupke • I Feel Pretty • Jet Song • Maria • One Hand One Heart • Prologue • The Rumble • Something's Coming • Somewhere • Somewhere (Ballet) • Tonight • Tonight (Ensemble)

CD 1067　GUYS AND DOLLS　PS88
• Adelaide's Lament • A Bushel and a Peck • Fugue for Tinhorns • Guys and Dolls • I'll Know • I've Never Been in Love Before • If I Were a Bell • Luck Be a Lady • Marry the Man Today • More I Cannot Wish You • Sit Down, You're Rockin' the Boat • Sue Me • Take Back Your Mink

CD 1016　LES MISERABLES/ PHANTOM OF THE OPERA　PS 419
• Bring Him Home • Castle On A Cloud • I Dreamed a Dream • On My Own • Stars • All I Ask Of You • The Music Of The Night • The Phantom Of The Opera • Think Of Me • Wishing You Were Somehow Here Again

The above listings are also available in a jewel box edition. The following are available in the jewel box edition only.

CD1121　BROADWAY HEROES & HEROINES .
The Party's Over . . . . .Judy Holliday
I Enjoy Being a Girl . . . . .Pat Suzuki
The Yankee Doodle Boy . . . . .George M. Cohan
I Won't Send Roses . . . .(Mack and Mabel)
If He Walked into My Life . . . .(Mame)
I Believe in You . . . . .How to Succeed in Business
Lucky to Be Me . . . .(On the Town)
Put on a Happy Face . . . .(Bye Bye Birdie)
Someone Else's Story . . . .(Chess)
Somewhere . . . .(West Side Story)
Time Heals Everything . . . .(Mack and Mabel)
Try to Remember . . . .(Fantasticks)

CD1162　SEND IN THE CLONES
Summer Wind . . . . .Frank Sinatra
Unforgettable .Nat Cole/Natalie Cole
You'll Never Find another Love . . . . .Lou Rawls
It Had to Be You . . . . .Harry Connick
As Time Goes By .Jimmy Durante
Up On the Roof . . . . .James Taylor
Something to Talk About . . . . .Bonnie Raitt
With One Look . . . . .Barbra Streisand
I Will Always Love You . . . . .Whitney Houston
Wind Beneath My Wings . . . . .Bette Midler

Welcome to MUSIC MINUS ONE compact discs and cassette tapes. Since 1951, MUSIC MINUS ONE has provided the professional and amateur musician with the finest, most extensive library of play-along and sing-along cassette tapes and compact discs in the world. Our catalog of over 250 compact discs and 700 cassette editions contains some of world's best and most requested musical literature.

In introducing compact discs into the Music Minus One product line, we added to most recordings a first-chair soloist on the right channel for your reference. This valuable feature will familiarize the student with the composition and performance. Additionally, we include the complete stereo orchestral background, minus the lead instrument, or voice, for your own performances. A complete performance score is included with each recording. Professionals and students are now able to practice with a complete orchestra right in their own home. What a great way to learn!

We are constantly in the process of recording works that you have requested throughout the years. Take a look at some of the great new recordings and instructional methods available.

CLARINET

MOZART Concerto, in A ....MMO CD 3201
WEBER Con. No. 1 in Fm, STAMITZ Con. No. 3 in Bb......MMO CD 3202
SPOHR Concerto No. 1 in C Minor Op. 26 ....MMO CD 3203
WEBER Con. Op. 26, BEETHOVEN Trio Op. 11...............MMO CD 3204
First Chair Clarinet Solos ....MMO CD 3205
The Art Of The Solo Clarinet: ....MMO CD 3206
MOZART Quintet in A, K.581 ....MMO CD 3207
BRAHMS Sonatas Op. 120 No. 1 & 2................................MMO CD 3208
WEBER Grand Duo Concertant WAGNER Adagio ....MMO CD 3209
SCHUMANN Fantasy Op. 73, 3 Romances Op. 94............MMO CD 3210
Easy Clarinet Solos Volume 1   Student Level..................MMO CD 3211
Easy Clarinet Solos Volume 2   Student Level..................MMO CD 3212
Easy Jazz Duets   Student Level..................MMO CD 3213

Classical concert cameos for clarinet, performed by two First-Chair players, and a recitalist. A broad array of pieces from the repertoire, covering 19th and 20th century composers, graded for difficulty, with commentary as to "how best to play these pieces."

Jerome Bunke, Clinician - Beginning Level........................MMO CD 3221
Harold Wright, Boston Symphony - Beginning Level.......MMO CD 3222
Stanley Drucker, NY Philharmonic - Intermediate Level...MMO CD 3223
Jerome Bunke, Clinician - Intermediate Level ....MMO CD 3224
Stanley Drucker, NY Philharmonic - Intermediate Level...MMO CD 3225
Harold Wright, Boston Symphony - Advanced Level ....MMO CD 3226
Stanley Drucker, NY Philharmonic - Intermediate Level...MMO CD 3227
Stanley Drucker, NY Philharmonic - Advanced Level ....MMO CD 3228
Harold Wright, Boston Symphony - Advanced Level ....MMO CD 3229

PIANO

BEETHOVEN Concerto No. 1 in C ....MMO CD 3001
BEETHOVEN Concerto No. 2 in Bb ....MMO CD 3002
BEETHOVEN Concerto No. 3 in C Minor ....MMO CD 3003
BEETHOVEN Concerto No. 4 in G ....MMO CD 3004
BEETHOVEN Concerto No. 5 in Eb ....MMO CD 3005
GRIEG Concerto in A Minor Op.16 ....MMO CD 3006
RACHMANINOFF Concerto No. 2 in C Minor ....MMO CD 3007
SCHUMANN Concerto in A Minor ....MMO CD 3008
BRAHMS Concerto No. 1 in D Minor ....MMO CD 3009
CHOPIN Concerto No. 1 in E Minor Op.11 ....MMO CD 3010
MENDELSSOHN Concerto No. 1 in G Minor ....MMO CD 3011
MOZART Concerto No. 9 in Eb K.271 ....MMO CD 3012
MOZART Concerto No. 12 in A K.414 ....MMO CD 3013
MOZART Concerto No. 20 in D Minor K.466 ....MMO CD 3014
MOZART Concerto No. 23 in A K.488 ....MMO CD 3015
MOZART Concerto No. 24 in C Minor K.491 ....MMO CD 3016
MOZART Concerto No. 26 in D K.537, "Coronation" ...MMO CD 3017
MOZART Concerto No. 17 in G K.453 ....MMO CD 3018
LISZT Concerto No. 1 in Eb, WEBER Op. 79 ....MMO CD 3019
LISZT Concerto No. 2 in A, Hungarian Fantasia ......MMO CD 3020
J.S. BACH Concerto in F Minor,J.C. BACH Con. in Fh ...MMO CD 3021
J.S. BACH Concerto in D Minor ....MMO CD 3022
HAYDN Concerto in D ....MMO CD 3023
Heart Of The Piano Concerto ....MMO CD 3024
Themes From Great Piano Concerti ....MMO CD 3025
TSCHAIKOVSKY Concerto No. 1 in Bb Minor ....MMO CD 3026
RACHMANINOFF 6 Scenes - 4 Hands ....MMO CD 3027
ARENSKY 6 Pieces/STRAVINSKY 3 Dances - 4 Hands ..MMO CD 3028
FAURE Dolly suite - 4 Hands ....MMO CD 3029
SCHUMANN Pictures From The East - 4 Hands ......MMO CD 3031
BEETHOVEN 3 Marches Op. 45 - 4 Hands ....MMO CD 3032

INSTRUCTIONAL METHODS

EVOLUTION OF THE BLUES ....MMO CD 7004
THE MUSIC TEACHER Basic Music Theory ....MMO CD 7002
RUTGERS UNIVERSITY MUSIC DICTATION SERIES ....MMO CD 7001
Over seven hours of intensive study in the fundamentals of music, basic musicianship, ear-training and sight reading. Now in use in over 3,000 universities, countless high schools and by individuals throughout the world. Paced for easy learning with test materials enclosed, This course is ideal for musicians and singers; invaluable for chorus. Available as seven compact discs or five cassettes in deluxe container.
List price: $98.50 per deluxe set   Please specify CDs or Cassettes

VIOLIN

BRUCH Concerto No. 1 in G Minor Op.26 ....MMO CD 3100
MENDELSSOHN Concerto in E Minor ....MMO CD 3101
TSCHAIKOVSKY Concerto in D Op. 35 ....MMO CD 3102
BACH Double Concerto in D Minor ....MMO CD 3103
BACH Concerto in A Minor, Concerto in E..........................MMO CD 3104
BACH Brandenburg Concerti Nos. 4 & 5 ....MMO CD 3105
BACH Brandenburg Concerto No. 2,Triple Concerto..........MMO CD 3106
BACH Concerto in Dm,(from Concerto for Harpsichord)...MMO CD 3107
BRAHMS Concerto in D Op. 77..............................MMO CD 3108
CHAUSSON Poeme, SCHUBERT Rondo..........................MMO CD 3109
LALO Symphonie Espagnole ....MMO CD 3110
MOZART Con. in D K.218, VIVALDI Con. Am Op.3 No.6....MMO CD 3111
MOZART Concerto in A K. 219..............................MMO CD 3112
WIENIAWSKI Con. in D, SARASATE Zigeunerweisen........MMO CD 3113
VIOTTI Concerto No.22 ....MMO CD 3114
BEETHOVEN 2 Romances, Sonata No. 5 in F "Spring"....MMO CD 3115
SAINT-SAENS Introduction & Rondo,
MOZART Serenade K. 204, Adagio K.261 ....MMO CD 3116
BEETHOVEN Concerto in D Op. 61(2 CD set).....................MMO CD 3117
The Concertmaster ....MMO CD 3118
Air On A G String (Favorite Encores w/Orchestra) ....MMO CD 3119
Concert Pieces for the Serious Violinist..............................MMO CD 3120
18th Century Violin Pieces ....MMO CD 3121
Orchestral Favorites Volume 1 - Easy Level ....MMO CD 3122
Orchestra Favorites Volume 2 - Medium Level..................MMO CD 3123
Orchestral Favorites Volume 3 - Med to Difficult Level......MMO CD 3124
The Three B's-Bach/Beethovan/Brahms..............................MMO CD 3125
VIVALDI Concerto in A Minor Op. 3 No. 6, in D Op. 3 No. 9,
Double Concerto Op. 3 No. 8 ....MMO CD 3126
VIVALDI - THE FOUR SEASONS (2 CD set) ....MMO CD 3127
VIVALDI Con. in Eb Op. 8 No. 5, ALBINONI Con. in A........MMO CD 3128
VIVALDI Concerto. in E Op. 3 No. 12,
Concerto in C Op. 8 #6 "Il Piacere" ....MMO CD 3129
SCHUBERT Three Sonatinas ....MMO CD 3130
HAYDN String Quartet Op. 76 No..............................MMO CD 3131
HAYDN String Quartet Op. 76 No. 2..............................MMO CD 3132
HAYDN String Quartet Op. 76 No. 3 "Emperor"................MMO CD 3133
HAYDN String Quartet Op. 76 No. 4 "Sunrise" ....MMO CD 3134
HAYDN String Quartet Op. 76 No. 5..............................MMO CD 3135
HAYDN String Quartet Op. 76 No. 6..............................MMO CD 3136

CELLO

DVORAK Concerto in B Minor Op.104 ....MMO CD 3701
C. P .E. BACH Concerto in A Minor ....MMO CD 3702
BOCCHERINI Concerto in Bb, BRUCH Kol Nidrei..............MMO CD 3703

OBOE

ALBINONI Concerti in Bb, Op. 7 No. 3, D Op. 7 No. 6,
D Minor Op. 9 No.2..............................MMO CD 3400
TELEMANN Concerto in Fm, HANDEL Concerto No. 8 in Bb,
VIVALDI Concerto No. 9 in Dm..............................MMO CD 3401
MOZART Quartet in F K. 370,
STAMITZ Quartet in F Op. 8 No. 3 ....MMO CD 3402
BACH Brandenburg Concerto No. 2,
TELEMANN Con. in Am ....MMO CD 340

GUITAR

BOCCHERINI Quintet No. 4 in D "Fandango" ....MMO CD 3601
GIULIANI Quintet in A Op. 65..............................MMO CD 3602
Classical Guitar Duets ....MMO CD 3603
Renaissance & Baroque Guitar Duets ....MMO CD 3604
Classical & Romantic Guitar Duets ....MMO CD 3605
Guitar and Flute Duets Vol. 1..............................MMO CD 3606
Guitar and Flute Duets Vol. 2..............................MMO CD 3607
Bluegrass Guitar ....MMO CD 3608

FLUTE

MOZART Concerto No. 2 in D, QUANTZ Concerto in G ....MMO CD 3300
MOZART Concerto in G K. 313..............................MMO CD 3301
BACH Suite No. 2 in B Minor ....MMO CD 3302
BOCCHERINI Concerto in D, VIVALDI Concerto in G Minor "La Notte",
MOZART Andante for Strings ....MMO CD 3303
HAYDN Divertimento, VIVALDI Concerto in D Op.10 No. 3 "Bullfinch",
FREDERICK THE GREAT Concerto in C ....MMO CD 3304
VIVALDI Concerto in F; TELEMANN Concerto in D, LECLAIR,
Concerto in C..............................MMO CD 3305
BACH Brandenburg No. 2 in F, HAYDN Concerto in D.......MMO CD 3306
BACH Triple Concerto, VIVALDI Concerto in D Minor ....MMO CD 3307
MOZART Quartet in F, STAMITZ Quartet in F..................MMO CD 3308
HAYDN 4 London Trios for 2 Flutes & Cello......................MMO CD 3309
BACH Brandenburg Concerti Nos. 4 & 5 ....MMO CD 3310
MOZART 3 Flute Quartets in D, A and C..........................MMO CD 3311
TELEMANN Suite in A Minor, GLUCK Scene from Orpheo,
PERGOLESI Concerto in G ....MMO CD 3312
FLUTE SONG: Easy Familiar Classics ....MMO CD 3313
VIVALDI Concerti In D RV 427, in G RV 438,
F Op. 10 No. 5..............................MMO CD 3314
VIVALDI Concerti in A Minor, RV 440,
G Op.10 No.4, D RV 429..............................MMO CD 3315
Easy Flute Solos Volume 1 ....MMO CD 3316
Easy Flute Solos Volume 2 ....MMO CD 3317
Easy Jazz Duets for Flute ....MMO CD 3318
Flute and Guitar Duets Vol. 1..............................MMO CD 3319
Flute and Guitar Duets Vol. 2..............................MMO CD 3320
First Chair Flute Solos with Orchestra ....MMO CD 3333

Four famous flutists perform frequently played pieces from the various
state lists. Levels of various difficulty are provided, and a master class
ensues as each player provides a performance guide in each flute
book.
Murray Panitz, Philadelphia Orch– Beginning Level ....MMO CD 3321
Donald Peck, Chicago Sym. Orch–Beginning Level ....MMO CD 3322
Julius Baker, N.Y. Philharmonic–Intermediate Level ....MMO CD 3323
Donald Peck, Chicago Symphony– Intermediate Level .....MMO CD 3324
Murray Panitz, Philadelphia Orchestra–Advanced Level ...MMO CD 3325
Julius Baker, N.Y. Philharmonic– Advanced Level.............MMO CD 3326
Donald Peck, Chicago Symphony– Intermediate Level .....MMO CD 3327
Murray Panitz, Philadelphia Orchestra–Advanced Level ...MMO CD 3328
Julius Baker, N.Y. Philharmonic–Intermediate Level ....MMO CD 3329
Doriot Anthony Dwyer, Boston Symphony–Beginning ....MMO CD 3330
Doriot Anthony Dwyer, Boston Symphony–Intermediate MMO CD 3331
Doriot Anthony Dwyer, Boston Symphony–Advanced......MMO CD 3332

FRENCH HORN

MOZART Concerti No.2 & No.3 in Eb, K. 417 & 447..........MMO CD 3501
Baroque Brass and Beyond ....MMO CD 3502
Music For Brass Ensemble ....MMO CD 3503

Nine programs for the French Horn, graded and performed by three
of the foremost hornists in the land. Programs across two centuries of
music, including both household names and modern contemporary
composers. A challenge for every player, graded for difficulty of per-
formance. Each player has commented upon his approach to the selec-
tions in the accompanying solo part book provided. A master class!
Mason Jones, Philadelphia Orchestra–Beginning Level....MMO CD 3511
Myron Bloom, Cleveland Symphony–Beginning Level .....MMO CD 3512
Dale Clevenger, Chicago Symphony–Intermediate Level ..MMO CD 3513
Mason Jones, Philadelphia Orchestra–Intermediate LevelMMO CD 3514
Myron Bloom, Cleveland Symphony– Advanced Level.....MMO CD 3515
Dale Clevenger, Chicago Symphony–Advanced Level.......MMO CD 3516
Mason Jones, Philadelphia Orchestra–Intermediate LevelMMO CD 3517
Myron Bloom, Cleveland Symphony–Advanced Level......MMO CD 3518
Dale Clevenger, Chicago Symphony–Intermediate Level ..MMO CD 3519

TRUMPET

3 Concerti, Haydn, Telemann, Fasch	MMO CD 3801
Trumpet Solos Vol. 1 - Student Edition	MMO CD 3802
Trumpet Solos Vol. 2 - Student Edition	MMO CD 3803
Easy Jazz Duets for Trumpet	MMO CD 3804
Music For Brass Ensemble	MMO CD 3805
First Chair Trumpet Solos	MMO CD 3806
The Art of the Solo Trumpet	MMO CD 3807
Baroque Brass and Beyond	MMO CD 3808
The Arban Duets	MMO CD 3809
Sousa Marches & Others	MMO CD 3810

Tune up your trumpet, as a trio of First-Chair men tackle the State Contest repertoire for this instrument, joined by a classical clinician of the first rank. Each CD is graded, carries a solo part booklet and a performance guide by each player. Tour the trumpet world with the best.

Gerard Schwarz, N.Y. Philharmonic - Beginning Level	MMO CD 3811
Armando Ghitalia, Boston Symphony - Beginning Level	MMO CD 3812
Robert Nagel, Soloist, NY Brass Ensemble–Intermediate	MMO CD 3813
Gerard Schwarz, N.Y. Philharmonic–Intermediate Level	MMO CD 3814
Robert Nagel, Soloist, NY Brass Ensemble–Advanced	MMO CD 3815
Armando Ghitalla, Boston Symphony–Intermediate	MMO CD 3816
Gerard Schwarz, N.Y. Philharmonic–Intermediate Level	MMO CD 3817
Robert Nagel, Soloist, NY Brass Ensemble– Advanced	MMO CD 3818
Armando Ghitalla, Boston Symphony–Advanced Level	MMO CD 3819
Raymond Crisara, Concert Soloist–Beginning Level	MMO CD 3820
Raymond Crisara, Concert Soloist–Beginning Level	MMO CD 3821
Raymond Crisara, Concert Soloist– Intermediate Level	MMO CD 3822

TROMBONE

Trombone Solos Vol. 1 - Student Edition	MMO CD 3901
Trombone Solos Vol. 2 - Student Edition	MMO CD 3902
Easy Jazz Duets for Trombone	MMO CD 3903

Three trombonists tour the repertoire for their instrument. Two, first-chair players; the third a "professor." Time to tune up your trombone and join the tour. Includes annotated solo parts plus suggestions for performance.

Per Brevig, Metropolitan Opera Orch. - Beginning Level	MMO CD 3911
Jay Friedman, Chicago Symphony - Beginning Level	MMO CD 3912
Keith Brown, Professor, Indiana University - Intermediate	MMO CD 3913
Jay Friedman, Chicago Symphony - Intermediate	MMO CD 3914
Keith Brown, Professor, Indiana University - Intermediate	MMO CD 3915
Per Brevig, Metropolitan Opera - Advanced Level	MMO CD 3916
Keith Brown, Professor, Indiana University - Advanced	MMO CD 3917
Jay Friedman, Chicago Symphony - Advanced Level	MMO CD 3918
Per Brevig, Metropolitan Opera - Advanced Level	MMO CD 3919

DOUBLE BASS

MASTER CLASS - The choicest repertoire for the Double Bass, performed by first chair soloists and then by YOU. Graded for easy selection, these include annotated solo parts plus suggestions for performance. Featuring: David Walter - soloist and Judith Olson - pianist.

Beginning to Intermediate Level	MMO CD 4301
Intermediate to Advanced Level	MMO CD 4302
Trios, Quartets, Quintets, Jazz Rock, Latin Studies	MMO CD 4303
The Beat Goes On - Jazz-Funk, Latin, Pop-Rock	MMO CD 4304
Bass-ic Rock	MMO CD 4305
Time-Less - 70s Style - Minus Bass	MMO CD 4306

TENOR SAX

Tenor Saxophone Solos Vol. 1 - Student Edition	MMO CD 4201
Tenor Saxophone Solos Vol. 2 - Student Edition	MMO CD 4202
Easy Jazz Duets for Tenor Saxophone	MMO CD 4203
For Saxes Only –Arranged by Bob Wilber	MMO CD 4204

ALTO SAXOPHONE

Alto Saxophone Solos Vol. 1 - Student Edition	MMO CD 4101
Alto Saxophone Solos Vol. 2 - Student Edition	MMO CD 4102
Easy Jazz Duets for Alto Saxophone	MMO CD 4103
For Saxes Only Arranged Bob Wilber	MMO CD 4104

Two of the foremost practitioners of this instrument solo to demonstrate proper intonation, attack and technique for this "Johnny-come-lately" to the legitimate world of classical music. Vincent Abato, a legend for his purity of tone and ability; and the foremost clinician in Canada on his instrument, Paul Brodie, provide a guide to the best in concert repertoire drawn from the various State Contest lists. Selections that each Alto Saxophonist must perform, to be graded.

Paul Brodie, Canadian Soloist - Beginning Level	MMO CD 4111
Vincent Abato, Metropolitan Orch. - Beginning Level	MMO CD 4112
Paul Brodie, Canadian Soloist - Intermediate Level	MMO CD 4113
Vincent Abato, Metropolitan Opera - Intermediate Level	MMO CD 4114
Paul Brodie, Canadian Soloist - Advanced Level	MMO CD 4115
Vincent Abato, Metropolitan Opera - Advanced Level	MMO CD 4116
Paul Brodie, Canadian Soloist - Advanced Level	MMO CD 4117
Vincent Abato, Metropolitan Opera - Advanced Level	MMO CD 4118

DRUMS

Four extraordinary Drum albums, by the Dean of American Jazz Drum Teachers, Jim Chapin. From the 'seminal drum book' Modern Jazz Drumming, now in its 23rd printing, through three Big Band and Small Combo Albums, Jim takes you into the history of jazz stylings that began with Gene Krupa's "Sing, Sing, Sing" solo thru the classic "Wipe Out" of the Ventures. A drummers collection to have and to treasure.

Modern Jazz Drumming - (2 CD set)	MMO CD 5001
For Drummers Only	MMO CD 5002
Wipe Out	MMO CD 5003
Sit-In with Jim Chapin	MMO CD 5004
Drum Star	MMO CD 5005
DRUMPADSTICKSKIN	MMO CD 5006
Classical Percussion, 2CD Set	MMO CD 5009

VOCAL

The following listing of vocal albums, for the serious student and professional singer, feature the world renowned accompanist, John Wustman. Among the many artists he has accompanied in past years have included: Jan Peerce, Roberta Peters, and the favorite of millions, Luciano Pavarotti.

All vocal editions feature only accompaniment tracks to allow full interpretation and flexibility for your vocal studies.

SCHUBERT German Lieder-High Voice, Vol.1 ....MMO CD 4001
SCHUBERT German Lieder-Low Voice, Vol.1 ....MMO CD 4002
SCHUBERT German Lieder-High Voice, Vol. 2 ....MMO CD 4003
SCHUBERT German Lieder-Low Voice, Vol. 2 ....MMO CD 4004
BRAHMS German Lieder-High Voice ....MMO CD 4005
BRAHMS German Lieder-Low Voice ....MMO CD 4006
Everybody's Favorite Songs-High Voice, Vol.1...................MMO CD 4007
Everybody's Favorite Songs-Low Voice, Vol.1 ....MMO CD 4008
Everybody's Favorite Songs-High Voice, Vol. 2.................MMO CD 4009
Everybody's Favorite Songs-Low Voice, Vol. 2 ....MMO CD 4010
17th/18th Cent. Italian Songs-High Voice, Vol.1 ....MMO CD 4011
17th/18th Cent. Italian Songs-Low Voice, Vol.1 ....MMO CD 4012
17th/18th Cent. Italian Songs-High Voice, Vol. 2 ....MMO CD 4013
17th/18th Cent. Italian Songs-Low Voice, Vol. 2 ....MMO CD 4014
Famous Soprano Arias ....MMO CD 4015
Famous Mezzo-Soprano Arias ....MMO CD 4016
Famous Tenor Arias...MMO CD 4017
Famous Baritone Arias...MMO CD 4018
Famous Bass Arias ....MMO CD 4019
WOLF German Lieder For High Voice ....MMO CD 4020
WOLF German Lieder For Low Voice ....MMO CD 4021
STRAUSS German Lieder For High Voice ....MMO CD 4022
STRAUSS German Lieder For Low Voice ....MMO CD 4023
SCHUMANN German Lieder For High Voice........................MMO CD 4024
SCHUMANN German Lieder For Low Voice ....MMO CD 4025
MOZART Arias For Soprano..MMO CD 4026
VERDI Arias For Soprano...MMO CD 4027
ITALIAN Arias For Soprano ....MMO CD 4028
FRENCH Arias For Soprano...MMO CD 4029
ORATORIO Arias For Soprano ....MMO CD 4030
ORATORIO Arias For Alto ....MMO CD 4031
ORATORIO Arias For Tenor ....MMO CD 4032
ORATORIO Arias For Bass ....MMO CD 4033

Master Class - The choicest repertoire for the vocalist. Professional artists sing these pieces to guide the singer in interpreting them.

Beginning Soprano Solos - Kate Hurney ....MMO CD 4041
Intermediate Soprano Solos - Kate Hurney........................MMO CD 4042
Beginning Mezzo Soprano Solos - Fay Kittelson................MMO CD 4043
Intermediate Mezzo Soprano Solos - Fay Kittelson............MMO CD 4044
Advanced Mezzo Soprano Solos - Fay Kittelson ....MMO CD 4045
Beginning Contralto Solos - Carline Ray ....MMO CD 4046
Beginning Tenor Solos - George Shirley ....MMO CD 4047
Intermediate Tenor Solos - George Shirley ....MMO CD 4048
Advanced Tenor Solos - George Shirley..............................MMO CD 4049

Pocket Songs
YOU SING THE HITS